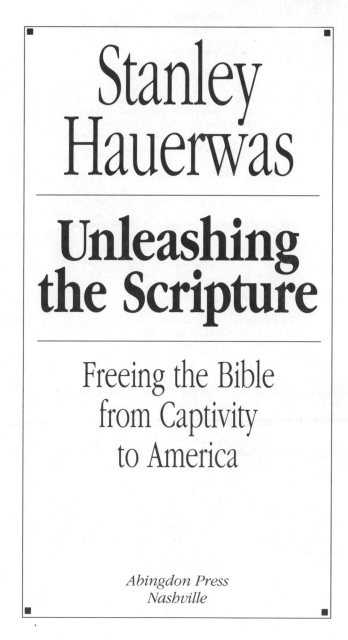

Stanley Hauerwas

Unleashing the Scripture

Freeing the Bible from Captivity to America

Abingdon Press
Nashville

Unleashing the Scripture:
Freeing the Bible from Captivity to America

Copyright © 1993 by Abingdon Press

93 94 95 96 97 98 99 00 01 02 — 10 9 8 7 6 5 4 3 2 1

This book is printed on recycled, acid-free paper.

Library of Congress Cataloging–in–Publication Data

Hauerwas, Stanley, 1940–
    Unleashing the scripture : freeing the Bible from captivity to America / Stanley Hauerwas.
        p.   cm.
    Includes bibliographical references.
    ISBN 0-687-31678-2 (alk. paper)
        1. Democracy—Religious aspects—Christianity. 2. Bible–Hermeneutics. 3. Modernist-fundamentalist controversy. I. Title.
BR115.P7H365 1993
220'.0973—dc20   93-11107
                                                                          CIP

Scripture quotations are from the New Revised Standard Version of the Bible, copyright © 1989 by the Division of Christian Education of the National Council of the Churches of Christ in the USA. Used by permission.

The quote on pp. 73-74 is from *The Shaking of the Foundations* by Paul Tillich. Copyright © 1948 by Charles Scribner's & Sons. Copyright renewed © 1976 by Hannah Tillich. Reprinted with permission of Charles Scribners, an imprint of Macmillan.

MANUFACTURED IN THE UNITED STATES OF AMERICA

To
Grady and Rowena Hardin,
Patsy and Will Willimon,
Herb and Susan Allred,
Faithful Preachers and Hearers

Contents

My work is often described as "provocative," "outrageous," and sometimes careless. I do not relish such descriptions, though I may deserve each of them. The latter description derives partly from my refusal to be an "ethicist." Rather I understand myself to be a theologian ranging over a wide array of topics. Some of these topics may be construed as ethics, but many could also be described as issues in New Testament or democratic theory. I simply am not interested in "careful" theology if that means avoiding the risk of writing about Christian convictions and practices as if they do not matter. Indeed, I believe that many of the disciplinary divisions characteristic of contemporary university and seminary curricula are but excuses for intellectual laziness or cowardice, or both.

Because this book resists the higher-critical method as the method for study of Scripture, it will earn further easy dismissals. Most people will label and dismiss me as fideistic, sectarian, tribalist. I obviously am not familiar with all current historical-critical studies of various parts of the Bible and will therefore be accused of lacking "expertise" or of unfairly stereotyping the diversity of the practice of historical criticism—"Does he not know about the turn to literary criticism, social criticism, rhetorical criticism, and so on." I certainly have learned from historical-critics, whose work I often think better than their theory. I am moreover aware that if I had known about X's or Y's study of Paul, I might need to qualify some of my claims or rewrite some of the exhibits. Yet one of the purposes of this book is to free those who preach and those who hear from thinking that we must rely on the latest biblical study if we are to proclaim the gospel.

It will be obvious from the following treatise and

exhibits that the Church's practices impede our ability to faithfully proclaim and hear the Scripture. Our failure to understand what Paul "really meant" is not the problem. Our problem is that we live in churches that have no practice of nonviolence, of reconciliation, no sense of the significance of singleness; so we lack the resources to faithfully preach and hear God's Word. If such an approach means that I risk being "unscholarly," it is a risk well worth taking in order to free theology from its academic captivity.

What I do could be of interest to other "academic" theologians and even Scripture scholars. Yet the audience I most want to reach is those who preach and listen Sunday after Sunday. That task is difficult because I am an academic and have been trained to write theology primarily for other theologians. Academic dialogue, of course, is an elite enterprise for those so skilled, but it bothers me that in so writing we fail to be accountable to the elite of the Church we call the saints.

The issue of audience and genre cannot be separated. Indeed I believe that we live in a time when it is by no means clear what form theology ought to take. I have no innovative solutions to suggest. In this book I am trying to experiment by combining a discursive essay with sermonic exhibits. I think the exhibits contain my best theology, which means that the form and content of theology and sermons are integrally related. I do not think the sermons are easier or less academically demanding than my other work, but rather serve to suggest that Christian theology is not the display of abstract ideas. Theology should be a form of discourse that is meant to help us live more faithfully as Christians who are part of that community called Church.

Though I am less than happy with the hegemony of the historical-critical method for the study of Scripture, it will be clear that I think theologians are the primary culprit. To the extent that we abandoned Scripture as integral to the theological enterprise, we allowed the Scripture to be separated from Church-centered practice. I really do not know the "text" of the Bible well—all my theological formation took place in curricula shaped by Protestant liberalism. Yet such formation was more "biblical" than I suspected because I now think it an advantage to learn Scripture through the work of Aquinas, Luther, Calvin, Barth, and Yoder.

Whether this book is "provocative" or "outrageous" I leave to the reader's judgment. In his book *After the Fire: The Destruction of the Lancaster County Amish*, Randy-Michael Testa quotes Flannery O'Connor:

> When you can assume that your audience holds the same beliefs you do, you can relax a little and use some more normal means of talking to it; when you have to assume that it does not then you have to make your vision apparent by shock—to the hard of hearing you shout, and for the almost-blind, you draw large and startling figures.

I know it will come as a shock to most readers that our fundamental problem with hearing the Bible can be attributed to our having accommodated our lives to the presuppositions of liberal democracies. The failure of liberal democracies, of course, is not a new theme for me, but many will find "startling" the implications for our reading of the Scripture. I do not apologize for that kind of shock. Thus the primary contention of this book: *The Bible is not and should not be accessible to merely anyone, but rather it should only be made available to those who have undergone the hard discipline of existing as part of God's people.*

Without such disciples this book could not have been written. I am particularly grateful to Blacknall Presbyterian Church of Durham, North Carolina, for asking me to give the 1991 Blacknall Lectures. It proved an ideal context for combining sermons and lectures. Phil Kenneson, then a member of Blacknall and a good friend, has helped me think through these matters for many years. I am also grateful to the faculty, staff, and students at Union Theological Seminary in Richmond, Virginia, for making me their Sprunt Lecturer, which gave me the chance to develop the themes in this book further. Professor Doug Ottati was a gracious and intellectually stimulating host while I was at Union. I also learned much by offering some of this material as the Slater-Wilson Lectures at St. Paul School of Theology. I am particularly grateful to my friend Tex Sample for such engaging conversation while I was there. I am also obviously indebted to my colleagues and students at the Divinity School at Duke University where many of the sermons were preached. It was under the urging of Dr. Paula Gilbert, then head of York Chapel, that I was reminded of my responsibility to preach as a member of the faculty in a divinity school.

Jim Fodor, Richard Hays, John Berkman, David Matzko, and Will Willimon read the manuscript and made wonderful suggestions. I owe much to Professor Reinhard Hutter, who never lets me forget that the Scripture is God's word through the gift of the Holy Spirit. Professor Michael Cartwright, with Dr. Hutter, rightly asked by what authority I preach. I wish I had a good response to that troubling question.

Mrs. Wanda Dunn has done the typing and much else that makes this possible. Her critical good humor is a gift I cherish. Paul Franklyn and Don Baker of Abingdon Press have done their usual good editing. Paul's support for this project has been unwavering as he actually thinks theologians ought to care about the Church. Paula Gilbert's steadfast faith in God literally makes all the difference. Her love makes my life happy.

I finish this while on sabbatical at the National Humanities Center. Many will find this ironic, given the argument of this book. I would like to think, however, that the willingness of the Center to support a theologian, and in particular a theologian like me, is a witness to what a surprising God we worship.

PART ONE

THE POLITICS OF THE BIBLE:

Sola Scriptura as Heresy?

Taking the Bible Away from North American Christians

Most North American Christians assume that they have a right, if not an obligation, to read the Bible. I challenge that assumption. No task is more important than for the Church to take the Bible out of the hands of individual Christians in North America. Let us no longer give the Bible to all children when they enter the third grade or whenever their assumed rise to Christian maturity is marked, such as eighth-grade commencements. Let us rather tell them and their parents that they are possessed by habits far too corrupt for them to be encouraged to read the Bible on their own.

North American Christians are trained to believe that they are capable of reading the Bible without spiritual and moral transformation. They read the Bible not as Christians, not as a people set apart, but as democratic citizens who think their "common sense" is sufficient for "understanding" the Scripture. They feel no need to stand under the authority of a truthful community to be told how to read. Instead they assume that they have all the "religious experience" necessary to know what the Bible is about. As a result the Bible inherently becomes the ideology for a politics quite different from the politics of the Church.

Note, it is not an issue of whether the Bible should be read politically, but an issue of which politics should determine our reading as Christians. All reading is embedded in a politics, and avoiding politics is not something for which we can or should strive. Politics, for Christians, names the conversations between members of a community across time, which is necessary for the discovery of values in common. Such a politics involves the exercise of power and authority and the unending task of not making power an end in itself. The problem with the current politics surrounding the Bible is the unwillingness to acknowledge itself as a politics—exactly because the genius of liberal politics is to hide its hegemony in the name of ideals, such as freedom of the individual to read however he or she wishes.

To suggest that the Bible should be taken away from North American Christians will strike many as absurd. They may assume that I am not serious. Is it not the very hallmark of Christianity, particularly Protestant Christianity, to encourage people to read the Bible? I certainly believe that God uses the Scripture to help keep the Church faithful, but I do not believe, in the Church's current circumstance, that each person in the Church thereby is given the right to interpret the Scripture. Such a presumption derives from the corrupt egalitarian politics of democratic regimes, not from the politics of the Church. The latter, as I will try to show, knows that the "right" reading of Scripture depends on having spiritual masters who can help the whole Church stand under the authority of God's Word.

In his *Journals*, the Danish philosopher-theologian Søren Kierkegaard wrote:

> Fundamentally a reformation which did away with the Bible would now be just as valid as Luther's doing away with the Pope. All that about the Bible has developed a religion of learning and law, a mere distraction. A little of that knowledge has gradually percolated to the simplest classes so that no one any longer reads the Bible humanly.

As a result it does immeasurable harm; where life is concerned its existence is a fortification of excuses and escapes; for there is always something one has to look into first of all, and it always seems to know one had first of all to have the doctrine in perfect form before one can begin to live—that is to say, one never begins.

The Bible Societies, those vapid caricatures of missions, societies which like all companies only work with money and are just as mundanely interested in spreading the Bible as other companies in their enterprises; the Bible Societies have done immeasurable harm. Christendom has long been in need of a hero who, in fear and trembling, had the courage to forbid people to read the Bible. That is something quite as necessary as preaching against Christianity.[1]

Kierkegaard helps us see that the current controversies between fundamentalism and those that approach the Scripture using the methods of biblical criticism are, from this perspective, a parochial debate. Indeed literalist-fundamentalism and the critical approaches to the Bible are but two sides of the same coin, insofar as each assumes that the text should be accessible to anyone without the necessary mediation by the Church.[2] The reformation doctrine of *sola scriptura*, joined to the invention of the printing press and underwritten by the democratic trust in the intelligence of the "common person," has created the situation that now makes people believe that they can read the Bible "on their own."[3] That presumption must be challenged, and that is why the Scripture should be taken away from Christians in North America.

I am aware that this suggestion cannot help appearing authoritarian and elitist. I am not, however, particularly bothered by such characterizations, because I am challenging the very presumption that communities can exist without authority. From the perspective of liberal political practice, any authority appears "authoritarian." By offering a different account of how Scripture resides within a different practice of authority, I hope to avoid the unhappy alternative assumption that all exercises of power are "authoritarian."[4]

To direct attention to the "politics" of the Bible may, moreover, seem to ignore the work done in hermeneutical theory that has had such a prominent place in recent theology. I have certainly learned much from the resurgence of literary approaches for the interpretation of the Bible.[5] Yet I cannot pretend that this is another book that develops hermeneutical theory, since I think such theorizing too often continues to underwrite the assumption that interpretation is largely an apolitical task.[6] Indeed I suspect that hermeneutics becomes the preoccupation of theology when the text of Scripture is divorced from particular practices of the Church that make it make sense in the first place.

For example, I believe that the battle between literalistic fundamentalism and critical approaches to the Bible is the result of the abstraction of the text of the Bible from such practices. The fundamentalist and biblical critic share the assumption that the text of the Bible should make rational sense (to anyone), apart from the uses that the Church has for Scripture. Fundamentalism and biblical criticism seek to depoliticize the interpretation of Scripture on the grounds that the text has an objective meaning. The result for both is repoliticization of Scripture by giving unchecked power to some interpreters over Scripture without such power being justified. Why this battle is a peculiarly modern one I will demonstrate by calling attention to recent work in the politics of interpretation, and by describing the Bible's use in other Christian traditions.

2

Stanley Fish, the Pope, and the Bible

In his book *Is There a Text in This Class?*, Stanley Fish helps us understand why fundamentalism and biblical criticism are but two sides of the same coin when looked at from a political perspective. In his introduction Fish describes "how I stopped worrying and learned to love interpretation." Early in his own work Fish confesses he asked the question, "Is the reader or the text the source of the meaning?" That question assumes that the only entities in question are the text and the reader, both of whose independence and stability are assumed. Fish tries to avoid the New Critics' perspective, which alleges that the text creates its own meaning. He also discards emotivism, which alleges that the readers could make whatever they wished of the text. As an alternative he proposes that a critic's account of a literary work is a disguised report of the normative experience of all informed readers.[1] Such reports are disguised because a reader who presumes to be a critic would feel compelled to translate his or her experience into a vocabulary of critical principles that he or she self-consciously holds.

The problem with such a privileged status for the reader-as-critic, says Fish, is the continuing presumption that there is a text. We must acknowledge that texts themselves only emerge as the consequence of interpretive acts.[2] In simple terms, Fish suggests that a play by Shakespeare, read as "literature" in a freshman English class, is quite different from a Shakespeare play performed for the entertainment of the groundlings.[3] In like manner, the letters of Paul to the Corinthians are quite differently understood once they become Scripture and are located in relationship to the other letters of Paul in the New Testament as well as the Gospels.

Once Paul's letters become so constructed canonically, Paul becomes one interpreter among others of his letters. If Paul could appear among us today to tell us what he "really meant" when he wrote, for example, 1 Corinthians 13, his view would not necessarily count more than Gregory's or Luther's account of Corinthians. There simply is no "real meaning" of Paul's letters to the Corinthians once we understand that they are no longer Paul's letters but rather the Church's Scripture. Such examples remind us, according to Fish, that texts only exist in a continuing web of interpretive practices. Therefore we cannot ask how we ought to interpret the text because we then assume that the text exists prior to such interpretive strategies. We must acknowledge that interpretive strategies are already at work in shaping our reading, and hence our conception of what a text is.

In an interesting way, Fish helps us see that much of the discussion of hermeneutics is misplaced. For example, Werner Jeanrond suggests that "the aim of hermeneutical reflection is not to replace the actual act of reading a text or of looking at a work of art, rather it wishes to help improve such acts by considering the possibilities and limitations of human understanding."[4] That way of putting the matter presupposes that the text exists as a fact and that we simply need to know how better to explicate what the fact really means. Yet we must acknowledge that the text has no "real" meaning, and no real, abstract "human understanding" exists to constitute such meaning.

Many find themselves quite uncomfortable with such

claims as they fear the alternative is subjectivism or, in the worst case, relativism. Fish, however, argues that such alternatives are not necessary, once it is acknowledged that strategies of interpretation are not those of an independent agent facing an independent autonomous text, but those of an interpretative community of which the reader is but a member. As Fish notes, such interpretative communities are made up of those "who share interpretative strategies not for the reading but for the writing of texts, for constituting their properties. In other words, these strategies exist prior to the act of reading and therefore determine the shape of what is read rather than, as is usually assumed, the other way around."[5]

Jeff Stout nicely puts the matter when he says, "At the heart of the current debate over literary theory is the question of which normative aims one ought to have in studying literature. What begins seeming like a debate over the nature of meaning reveals itself before long as a struggle over what makes literature worth caring about and what kind of society to strive for."[6] Interpretation is not an objective science because, from beginning to end, it is an exercise in politics. It is not only about power and authority, but also about shared goods and judgments that constitute a history worth remembering for a people.

While Fish's and Stout's views strike many as dangerous, their ideas in fact share much with traditional Christian presuppositions. Consider why Stanley Fish and Pope John Paul II are on the same side when it comes to the politics of interpretation. Both men assume that the text, and in this case the text of Scripture, can be interpreted only in the context of an "interpretative community." For John Paul II (and all the apostles before him in the tradition), the community necessary for the reading of Scripture is the Roman Catholic Church, which includes the Office of the Magisterium.

For example, in the "Dogmatic Constitution on Divine Revelation," promulgated at Vatican II, we find the familiar claim: "It is not from sacred Scripture alone that the Church draws her certainty about everything which has been revealed. There both sacred tradition and sacred Scripture are to be accepted and venerated with the same sense of devotion and reverence."[7] Yet it is not simply that sacred tradition and sacred Scripture must be always read together but that they must be read as such by the Church. Thus, the Dogmatic Constitution continues:

> Sacred tradition and sacred Scripture form one sacred deposit of the word of God, which is committed to the Church. Holding fast to this deposit, the entire holy people united with their shepherds remain always steadfast in the teaching of the apostles, in the common life, in the breaking of bread, and in prayers (cf. Acts 2, 42), so that in holding to, practicing, and professing the heritage of the faith, there results on the part of the bishops and the faithful a remarkable common effort.
>
> The task of authentically interpreting the word of God, whether written or handed on, has been entrusted exclusively to the living teaching office of the Church, whose authority is exercised in the name of Jesus Christ. This teaching office is not above the word of God, but serves it, teaching only what has been handed on, listening to it devoutly, guarding it scrupulously, and explaining it faithfully by divine commission and with the help of the Holy Spirit; it draws from this one deposit of faith everything which it presents for belief as divinely revealed.
>
> It is clear, therefore, that sacred tradition, sacred Scripture, and the teaching authority of the Church, in accord with God's most wise design, are so linked and joined together that one cannot stand without the others, and that all together each in its own way under the action of the Holy Spirit contributes effectively to the salvation of the souls.[8]

From such a perspective it is obviously absurd to assert that Scripture can be self-interpreting. Rather, Scripture can be rightly interpreted only within the practices of a body of people constituted by the unity found in the Eucharist. The Roman Catholics conclude that any church cannot rightly read the Scripture if it is divided from itself in a way that makes it impossible for people to celebrate the Eucharist with one another in the union with Christ.[9] In like manner, any churches divided from Rome, which means they are divided from themselves, lack the ability to use faithfully Scripture for the whole Church.

Protestants often hear such claims as restrictive, arrogant, and authoritarian; in fact this doctrine is meant to effect the opposite reaction. Exactly because there is an office of unity more profound than a biblical text, Catholics can encourage many readings of Scripture.[10] For Catholics know that they are not only constituted by being Catholic in England, or France, and even the whole of Europe, but they are Catholic in Kenya, Argentina, and Burma as well. They assume that, of course, many different readings will come from such diversity. This diversity is not a problem, but rather necessary for the building up of the unity found in that church's practices. You do not have or need "a meaning" of the text when you understand that Church is more determinative than text.

The Roman Catholic Church, of course, does not exclude the possibility that historical and critical analysis of the Scriptures may prove to offer valuable, diverse readings. They simply refuse to privilege that method as the only one that can determine the meaning of the text. For they understand that it is not the "meaning of the text" that interests the Church but rather how the Spirit that is found in the Eucharist is also to be seen in Scripture. Thus they contend:

Since Holy Scripture must be read and interpreted according to the same Spirit by whom it was written, no less serious attention must be given to the content and unity of the whole of Scripture, if the meaning of the sacred text is to be correctly brought to light. The living tradition of the whole Church must be taken into account along with the harmony which exists between elements of the faith. It is the task of exegetes to work according to these rules toward a better understanding and explanation of the meaning of the sacred Scripture, so that through preparatory study the judgment of the Church may mature. For all of what has been said about the way of interpreting Scripture is subject finally to the judgment of the Church, which carries out the divine commission and ministry guarding and interpreting the word of God.[11]

Roman Catholics are not alone in their view of the necessity of Scripture to reside within churchly practice. The Orthodox are equally insistent that Scripture only makes sense within the traditions and practices of the Church. For example, Georges Florosky in *Bible, Church, Tradition: An Eastern Orthodox View* argues that obviously Scripture and tradition are insufficient in and of themselves as they were given only within the Church. Moreover it is only in the Church that they receive their fullness and value. It is not as if Scripture and tradition, according to Florosky, constitute the Church's witness but rather that Scripture and tradition reflect the prior reality of the Church. Therefore it is only in the Church that Scripture lives and becomes vivified: "only within the Church is it revealed as a whole and not broken up into separate texts, commandments, and aphorisms."[12]

Scripture cannot be self-sufficient, asserts Florosky, not because it is incomplete but because Scripture never claims to be self-sufficient. Employing the Orthodox sense of *eikon*, he suggests that Scripture is the image of truth but certainly not truth itself. "Strange to say, we often limit the freedom of the Church as a whole, for the sake of furthering the freedom of individual Christians."[13] So ironically, in the name of an abstract biblical standard, the individual consciousness is set free from the spiritual demands embodied in the experience of the Church. Thus, Florosky goes so far as to state what Protestant readers fear: "This is the denial of catholicity, a destruction of Catholic consciousness; this is the sin of the Reformation."[14] If Scripture is declared to be self-sufficient, it is only exposed to subjective and arbitrary interpretation—cut away, as it is, from its sacred source.

From the Orthodox perspective the Church, as the body of Christ, stands first and is more full than Scripture. This does not limit Scripture, but it reminds us that Christ appears before us not only in Scripture but in the Church. "In the time of early Christians the Gospels were not yet written and could not be the sole source of knowledge. The Church acted according to the spirit of the Gospel, and, what is more, the Gospel came to life in the Church, in the Holy Eucharist. In the Christ of the Eucharist, Christians learned to know Christ of the Gospels, and so His image became vivid to them."[15]

This brief review hardly does justice to the complexity of the relationship between text and community and in particular the relationship between the Church and its Scripture. However, I think that at least by calling attention to the communal presuppositions necessary for any account of the Christian use of Scripture, we can see how the debate between fundamentalists and biblical critics is really more a debate between friends who share many of the same assumptions. The most prominent shared assumption is that the interpretation of the biblical texts is not a political process involving questions of power and authority. By privileging the individual interpreter, who is thought capable of discerning the meaning of the text apart from the consideration of the good ends of a community, fundamentalists and biblical critics make the Church incidental.

That fundamentalists and biblical critics share this assumption should not be surprising, given the character of Protestant Christianity, whether it be liberal or conservative, in America. Consider G. Ernest Wright's lamentation in *The Biblical Doctrine of Man in Society:*

> But no matter how high the doctrine of the church to which a particular confession may adhere in actual practice its congregations are a gathering of individuals who know little of Christian community in the biblical sense and expect little from it. Like secular clubs they meet in their various groups to hear speakers on a variety of topics which are usually unrelated, undigested, and unillumined by the Christian faith. The Church's theology, traditionally so triumphantly and vigorously theocentric, tends now to be dominated by anthropology, by volume after volume like this one, on the nature of man and the basis of his social thought and action. The worship of the Church has been heavily influenced by individualistic pietism, concerned largely, not with the social organism, but with the individual's need of peace, rest and joy in the midst of the storms and billows of life. The self-centeredness of the pietistic search for salvation tends to exclude vigorous concern with community. Hence, the modern Christian searches his Bible in a manner not unlike the pagan's study of his sacred literature, the purpose being to find inspirational, devotional, and moral enlightenment for personal living, and nothing more. The sectarianism of the Churches, and their racial and national cleavages, are further expressions of an individualism which distorts the nature of Christian society and provides excuse for the world's individualism.[16]

It may be that the emphasis on the Church as the polity for reading and understanding Scripture fails to appreciate the importance that the Reformation placed on the authority of Scripture. The Reformers were rightly concerned that the Scripture act as a judge on the Church. *Sola scriptura* was, no doubt, an important form of protest against many of the normal readings that had so captured the imagination of the Church at the time of the Reformation. The problem now is not how *sola scriptura* was used by the Reformers but how it is used by us.[17]

For example, Gerhard Ebeling suggests in *The Word of God and Tradition,* that *sola scriptura* fulfills its essential function in the following ways:

> It preserves intact the *distinction between text and interpretation;* while the Catholic conception is in danger of ascribing to an interpretation the value of an authoritative text. Next, *sola scriptura* maintains that the Word of God has absolute authority over the Church which was brought into existence by the Word of God, and therefore, that the Church itself is not the authoritative source of the Word of God, a view which blurs the *distinction between the Word of God and the Church.* Lastly, *sola scriptura* maintains that Christ *remains distinct from the Church as its Head,* and that the Church is the result of and dependent on the event that constituted her as Church.[18]

When *sola scriptura* is used to underwrite the distinction between text and interpretation, then it seems clear to me that *sola scriptura* is a heresy rather than a help in the Church. When this distinction persists, *sola scriptura* becomes the seedbed of fundamentalism, as well as biblical criticism. It assumes that the text of the Scripture makes sense separate from a Church that gives it sense. Perhaps those among us who maintain such a position forget that for much of the Church's life most Christians could not read, but that did not in itself make them less faithful. That Christians have thought it possible to translate our Scriptures should be sign enough that no strong distinction can be made between text and interpretation. That Christians have learned of Christ and Christ's relationship to Israel through biblical scenes portrayed on church windows and stone carvings and statues of the saints, alive and dead, should be sufficient for us to realize that the text of the Scripture is not meant to be "preserved intact" separate from the Church. God certainly uses Scripture to call the Church to faithfulness, but such a call always comes in the form of some in the Church reminding others in the Church how to live as Christians—no "text" can be substituted for the people of God.

3

The Bible and America

If fundamentalism and biblical criticism are both aberrations in the Christian tradition, then we ask, "Why are we so beset by this option in contemporary Protestant life in America?"[1] The beginning of the answer is already contained in the thoughts of G. Ernest Wright. In the nineteenth century there was a strong relationship between American individualism and the claims for the Bible as the sole authority for Christians. In particular John W. Nevin called attention to the friendly relationship between the Bible and the "sects" (or denominations). He notes that the sects place great stress on the authority of the Bible as the only textbook and guide for their life. If the Bible is at once so clear and full as a source of Christian doctrine, how does it come to pass that people are divided from one another over how to interpret it? "We must either admit a limitation in some form of the principle, no creed but the Bible, or else make up our minds at once to the hard requirement of accepting this array of sects as the true and legitimate form of the Christian life, equally entitled to respect and confidence in all its parts."[2]

If we presume that the Bible is its own standard, if we claim "no creed but the Bible," then the authority of the Bible is not privileged. Instead the authority of our private judgment will prevail. "It is easy enough to see," says Nevin, "that the supreme authority of the Bible, as it is made to underline professedly the religion of all the sects, is tacitly, if not openly, conditioned always by the assumption that every man is authorized and bound to get at this authority in a direct way for himself, through the medium simply of his own single mind."[3]

North American fundamentalism is a complex phenomenon that actually arose independent of the development of biblical criticism. The nineteenth-century form of fundamentalism, according to George Marsden, is distinct because fundamentalists of all stripes thought of themselves as representing the intellectual and scientific approach to Scripture. They assumed that their literalistic approach to Scripture was driven by common sense and science because:

> The prevailing intellectual opinion in the nineteenth-century America was enamored of the "Common Sense" ideals of the Scottish Enlightenment, which provided an intellectual base for the unshakable faith in the inductive scientific method associated with the seventeenth-century philosopher Francis Bacon. The strength of these ideals is evidenced by the difficulties that Romantic and transcendentalist thinkers had in trying to displace them. "It is taken for granted," lamented James Marsh in introducing his important edition of Coleridge's *Aids to Reflection* in 1829, "that our whole system of philosophy of mind, as derived from Lord Bacon especially, is the only one which has any claims to common sense." Moreover, he said, this Baconian Common Sense system was so completely identified with Protestantism "that by most persons they are considered as necessary parts of the same system." Proponents of inductive scientific reasoning agreed. "Protestant Christianity and the Baconian philosophy originate in the same foundation," said Presbyterian philosopher Samuel Tyler. "There never could have been a Bacon without the Bible," concurred the Southern theologian Benjamin Morgan Palmer. "Francis Bacon was the offspring of the Reformation."[4]

We should not be surprised, therefore, that the Baconian fundamentalists were convinced that all they were doing was taking the hard facts of the Scripture and discovering the patterns that were simply there. Charles Hodge developed his *Systematic Theology* as if it were a scientific primer.

> If natural science be concerned with the facts and laws of nature, theology is concerned with the facts and the principles of the Bible. If the object of the one would be to arrange and systematize the facts of the external world, and to ascertain the laws by which they were determined; the object of the other is to systematize the facts of the Bible, and ascertain the principles or general truths which these facts involve.[5]

The fundamentalist approach to the scientific explication of Scripture continued the Protestant opposition to allegorical methods, which were considered an esoteric interpretation of Scripture. If the Scripture had spiritual meanings that were not immediately apparent, then people with common sense, who approached the reading of the Scripture on their own, could not be expected to discover those meanings. So this presumed scientific approach to Scripture underwrote the presumption that the person of common sense possesses the ability to understand the Scripture without further aid.

Once again, the fundamentalist has the same agenda as the liberal Protestant. For example, Nathan Hatch calls attention to the prominent Unitarian Noah Worcester, "who challenged people to think for themselves, to slough off a 'passive state of mind' that deferred to great names in theology. 'The scriptures,' he declared, 'were designed for the great mass of mankind and are in general adapted to their capacities.' "[6]

The claim that the meaning of the Scripture is plain, of course, goes hand in hand with the North American distrust of all forms of authority. To make the Bible accessible to anyone is to declare that clergy status is secondary. The Bible becomes the possession not of the Church but now of the citizen, who has every right to determine its meaning. Ironically, by freeing the Bible from the Church and putting it in the possession of the individual conscience, the Bible becomes, in the process, the possession of nationalistic ideologies.[7] America becomes a Christian nation sanctified by God.

It is not surprising that when fundamentalists confronted the developments of higher criticism, they assumed advocates of the latter were attacking not only the Bible but also the United States' identity as a Protestant nation. For, as Marsden notes, the commonsense tradition assumed that the rationality and morality that were characteristic of the American ethos were the products of this country's status as a Protestant nation. Yet exactly to the extent that that was assumed, fundamentalists had no way to account for the collapse of that consensus. As Marsden observes, fundamentalism "was very typically American. That is, it combined with its Christianity certain nineteenth-century American ideas about truth and morality. These values, as well as a traditional and biblical Christianity, had to be saved from the delusion of the critics. The intellectual, moral, and religious issues were too intertwined to be sorted out thoroughly."[8]

The fundamentalists were such rationalists that they assumed the higher critics represented something of a conspiracy of intellectuals. As Charles Blanchard put it, "Unbelief seems never to have originated with the common man." These biblical critics have arisen with their speculation about how to interpret Scripture because "the critics of our time have been usually men who have poisoned their nervous systems and injured their minds by the use of narcotics and other poisons." Rationalists to the end, fundamentalists can only assume that biblical critics are people under the influence.[9]

The irony of the fundamentalist attack on the higher critics is that higher critics shared many of the fundamentalist's presuppositions. In particular the higher critics, at least in their earliest manifestations, assumed that the text had a meaning that was not dependent on the community. In his article "The Superiority of Precritical Exegesis," David Steinmetz directs our attention to Benjamin Jowett's famous 1854 essay on the interpretation of Scripture. According to Jowett:

> Scripture has one meaning—the meaning which it had in the mind of the Prophet or Evangelist who first uttered or wrote, to the hearers or readers who first received it. Scripture could be interpreted like any other book, and later accretions and venerated traditions surrounding its interpretation should, for the most part, be brushed aside or severely discounted. "The true use of interpretation is to get rid of interpretation and leave us alone with the author." [10]

Jowett did not foresee great difficulties in the way of getting to the meaning which was in the mind of the author. Obviously interpretation requires imagination, the ability to put oneself in an alien situation, the knowledge of a language, and the history of an ancient people. In terms of the Bible, according to Jowett, one has to bear in mind the progressive nature of revelation—in particular the superiority of later religious insights to earlier ones. But Jowett believed that if the interpreters possess the proper linguistic tools, "universal truth easily breaks through the accidents of time and place" and such truth still speaks to the condition of the unchanging human heart. [11]

Critical biblical scholarship has changed enormously since Jowett's day and is changing even more rapidly as we near the end of the twentieth century. Few scholars today, says Steinmetz, would argue as Jowett did that through the reconstruction of the gospel we see Jesus as "a teacher speaking to a group of serious, but not highly educated, working men, attempting to inculcate in them a loftier and sweeter morality." Nevertheless Steinmetz argues that the difference between Jowett and modern biblical criticism is less a quarrel over Jowett's hermeneutical theory than it is a disagreement with him over the application of the theory to actual exegetical practice.[12]

For example, most scholars trained in biblical criticism still seek to recover the "original" historical context of the text, the original intention of the author, and they regard the exegetical tradition prior to the development of historical criticism as an obstacle to proper understanding of the true meaning of the text. As Steinmetz notes, many biblical critics still assume that "the most primitive meaning of the text is the valid meaning, and the historical critical method is the only key which can unlock it."[13] Thus Krister Stendahl, in his influential article on biblical interpretation in the *Interpreters Dictionary of the Bible*, argues that the biblical criticism could achieve clarity about its task if it recognized that biblical theology is a "descriptive discipline" and not a normative one—that is, biblical criticism seeks to describe what "it meant," not what "it means."[14] Stendahl grants that bias is unavoidable and critics certainly ought, in the introduction of their book, to expose their own peculiar presuppositions. However, as he puts it, "what is more important is that once we confine ourselves to the task of descriptive biblical theology as a field in its own right, the material itself gives us means to check whether our interpretation is correct or not."[15] For it is the task of the biblical critic "to find out what these words meant when uttered or written by the prophet, the priest, the evangelist, or the apostle" regardless of their meaning in latter stages of religious history, our own included.[16]

In an odd way we see operating in Stendahl's assumptions the same sets of commitments that fuel fundamentalism. Both want to make the text accessible to anyone without training. To be sure, biblical critics assume that intellectual training is necessary, because in order to be a biblical critic you must learn linguistic and historical skills as well as "the state of the interpretive art." Nevertheless, the competent historian is but the person of common sense who has now received a liberal university education. The political presupposition of that training is of course not avowed or disclosed.

Fundamentalists and biblical critics alike fail to acknowledge the political character of their account of the Bible, and they fail to do so for very similar reasons. They want to disguise how their "interpretations" underwrite the privileges of the constituency that they serve. Admittedly, such realities may also be hidden from themselves, convinced as they are of the "objectivity" of their method. Accordingly, fundamentalism and biblical criticism are Enlightenment ideologies in the service of the fictive agent of the Enlightenment—namely, the rational individual—who believes that truth in general (and particularly the truth of the Christian faith) can be known without initiation into a community that requires transformation of the self. In this sense, fundamentalism and biblical criticism are attempts to maintain the influence of Constantinian Christianity—now clothed in the power of Enlightenment rationality—in the interest of continuing Christianity's hegemony over the ethos of North American cultures. Fortunately or unfortunately, depending on your ecclesiology, America is a society that is increasingly learning that it can do well without Christian presuppositions and practices.

The biblical critic and fundamentalist of course simply serve different constituencies within the North American polity. The fundamentalist serves the lower and middle class; the biblical critic feeds on the semiliterate class associated with the university. Both wish to make Christianity available to the person of common sense without moral transformation. "All you need is to study these texts in order to discover their plain meaning." Both camps assume an objectivity of the text in order to make the Bible available to anyone, and that "anyone" is assumed to be the citizen of democratic polities.[17]

Fundamentalists and biblical critics alike argue that their project is to get to the text's "real meaning." But of course the text has no "real meaning"; rather the Scriptures are maintained by the Church as having particular prominence because Christians have learned that the Scriptures exist to further the practices of witness and conversion. If I deny that the text has "a meaning," some biblical scholars fear an uncontrollable subjectivism. Interpreters, especially laity, can simply make of the text anything that they wish, creating the meaning of the text at will. Such a presumption, however, as Fish pointed out above, assumes that the only entities involved are the text and the individual interpreter. Texts and interpreters, however, work only within contexts that make what they have to say irrelevant or interesting. What is required, then, is an account of how new readings help us extend our habits in ways not foreseen.

Of course the Church creates the meaning of Scripture, but that does not invite an orgy of subjectivistic arbitrariness. Rather the Church must continue to return to the Scriptures because they are so interesting, given the Church's task to live as a people of memory in a world without memory. The Church returns time and time again to Scripture not because it is trying to find the Scripture's true meaning, but because Christians believe that God has promised to speak through Scripture so that the Church will remain capable of living faithful by remembering well. The more interesting the challenges facing the Church, the more readings we will need. It is for this reason that the Church, through the guidance of the Holy Spirit, tests contemporary readings of Scripture against the tradition, knowing that such readings help us to see the limits of the present.

Those who concentrate on trying to discover the "real meaning" of the text overlook the fact that the Church is charged week after week to practice preaching. It is not as if preaching explicates the same invariant meaning of the text, applying it to different circumstances, but rather that preaching helps us see that what is at stake is not the question of "the meaning of Scripture," but the usefulness of Scripture, given the good ends of Christian community. The Scriptures are exhibited in communities that are capable of pointing to holy lives through which we can rightly see the reality that has made the Scriptures possible.

Contrast Athanasius' observation at the end of his *Incarnation of the Word of God* with theories of interpretation like fundamentalism and biblical criticism.

> For the searching and right understanding of the Scriptures there is need of a good life and pure soul, and for Christian virtue to guide the mind to grasp, so far as human nature can, the truth concerning God the Word. One cannot possibly understand the teaching of the saints unless one has a pure mind and is trying to imitate their life. Anyone who wants to look at sunlight naturally wipes his eye clean first, in order to make at any rate some approximation to the purity of that on which he looks; and a person wishing to see a city or country goes to the place in order to do so. Similarly, anyone who wishes to understand the mind of the sacred writers must first cleanse his own life, and approach the saints by copying their deeds. Thus united to them in fellowship of light, he will both understand the things revealed to them by God and therefore escaping the pale important centers in the judgment,

will receive that which was laid up for saints in the kingdom of heaven.[18]

According to Athanasius, any attempt to make Scripture intelligible in and of itself can only be seen as an attempt to protect ourselves from the challenge of having our lives changed. Such change means making our lives available to others who have begun such a transformation. In short, if we are to understand Scripture it is necessary that we place ourselves under authority, a placement that at least begins by our willingness to accept the discipline of the Church's preaching.

4

Political Preaching

It should be clear by now why this is not another book on the relationship between the Bible and ethics or even on the ethical use of Scripture. The academic divisions between Bible and ethics, which are legitimated by university and seminary curriculums, are merely indications of how completely the Church has been captured by an alien polity. I do not suggest that all attempts to explore the relationship between ethics and Scripture are misguided. Indeed Stephen Fowl and Gregory Jones in *Reading in Communion: Scripture and Ethics in the Christian Life* helpfully clarify the kind of politics that are necessary to resist the presumption that Scripture is a problem for people who are facing a "moral dilemma."[1] The presumption that we have such a "problem" is itself a creation of the politics of liberal Protestantism, which attempts to make the gospel relevant to the realities of democratic polities.[2]

Particularly helpful in this respect are those proposals for allegorical readings of the Scriptures. Such readings are unavoidable, says Rowan Greer, once the Church made the fateful decision—and perhaps the most important political decision ever made—that the worship of Jesus is unintelligible without the witness of the continuing presence of the Jews.

> The Church came to insist that the God of Israel was the God of Jesus Christ and also that the significance of the Hebrew Scriptures lay in the testimony they bore to Christ.

In the decision as to which Christian writing can be considered the apostolic witness to Christ is really a decision that these books interpreted Christ correctly from a theological point of view. For Christians, the dialogue between God and his people found its fullest expression in Christ, and so Christ became the key to the whole of Scripture. The theological and even christological convictions that determined how the Christian Bible was to be constituted then became central in shaping the interpretation of the Bible.[3]

The fundamental politics that determine the Church's use of Scripture is the ongoing argument that Jews and Christians must continue through history. Christians cannot avoid the reality that Jews embody God's promise to Abraham. Whether Jews can avoid the reality that Christians claim to worship the God of Abraham is not for me, a Christian, to say. Yet, as a Christian, I can say that to the extent that we have tried to become a "civilizational" religion, in contrast to the Jews, we have become deficient in the kind of training necessary to be a people who rightly have our lives constituted scripturally. Inevitably we thus lose the ability to see Christ prefigured in the Jewish tradition.

The use of allegory is the way Christians have acknowledged the multiple senses of Scripture.[4] This kind of appeal to allegory is useful as long as one remembers that allegory is not about an individual discerning deeper spiritual meaning—as if the text had such meaning in itself—but rather allegory is the attempt at the renarration of the text for the good ends of a community. Allegory is necessary for the Christian rereading of the Bible as the Church negotiates between Israel and the particular political challenges of the different cultures in which it finds itself.[5]

Allegory turns out to be the way a tradition develops by providing new readings that challenge the accepted readings from the past. Therefore allegory is not only a way of reading texts, according to David Dawson, but rather it is a way of using certain readings to reinterpret culture and society. Allegory is not so much a method, but rather names the constitution of fields on which the struggle between competing proposals for thought and action can be worked out. As Dawson says, "The very tensions between literal and nonliteral readings that characterize ancient allegory stem from efforts by readers to secure for themselves and their communities social and cultural identity, authority and power."[6]

Allegory cannot be reduced to a method. Ironically, in many ways the so-called "close reading" of the biblical text, much of it done by higher critics, has itself been a form of allegory. By helping us notice the overlooked word or phrase, close reading helps us discover fresh and timely readings. Such readings often are not simply attempts to get the text "right" but rather invitations, suggestions, and recommendations to help us get ourselves right—that is, they are meant to tell us what to do as Christians.

Therefore the rest of this book consists of sermons.[7] I have no illusions about my mastery of the art of sermons. I am not even sure that these exhibits (whether artful or not) remain sermons when they appear in print. They are perhaps best thought of as biblical lectures or readings, presupposing as they do a people who still care about the use of the Bible for their lives together.[8] Even with this disclaimer, however, I consider these sermonic exhibits the best examples I can put forth to display the implications for practicing what I preach.

The practice of preaching is just that—disciplined practice. I make no claims to be interpreting the Scripture in order to get at the "real meaning." The "meaning" is that use to which I put these texts for the upbuilding of the Church. The common theme running through these sermons is that Scripture only makes sense as the book of the Church. Thus

in the sermon "The Insufficiency of Scripture: Why Discipleship Is Required," I argue that discipleship is required for
the right reading of Scripture. I hope it will be clear that I
have tried to take seriously the lectionary texts assigned in
each of these sermons, but the sermon itself is not just an
exposition of the text. Rather it is a renarration of the text,
which assumes that no account of any text is truthful that is
not about God's care of God's creation through Israel and
the Church. A sermon is scriptural when it inscribes a community into an ongoing Christian narrative.

It may be objected that the problem with this method
for the display of the politics of preaching is that it is not
much of a method. That is certainly true. Indeed that is
why these sermons can only be exhibits. Part of the problem is the misguided attempt to substitute method for
examples. The gospel must produce itself through enact-
ment, or it will lack the power to form and move lives.

Each sermon is the result of contingent sets of circumstances. Some I remember, some I do not. Yet in a sense
they all presume that I am preaching to people who,
because they are Christians, know that they are different
from those who are not. For example, the sermon "Hating
Mothers Is the Way to Peace" was the result of a particular
combination of events that cannot be repeated, but I
believe those events created a context for a particularly useful reading of Luke 14. The sermon was written because I
was asked by one of my students to preach on a Sunday set
aside for reading the United Methodist Bishops' pastoral
letter on nuclear war, "In Defense of Creation." I simply
used the lectionary text for that day, and as a result I was
able to make a connection between Jesus' challenge to the
family and our continuing underwriting of war and nuclear
weapons as correlative to our "safety" as Americans.

Such anti-family texts are ignored within mainstream
contemporary Protestantism because of our commitment

to the politics of democratic society and its idolization of the family. No amount of reading of the text as text can challenge that form of politics. Unless the Church is constituted by a counterpolitics in which singleness is as valid a way of life as marriage, we will not be able to hear or preach the Church's apocalyptic judgment on this family.[9] We will not be able to do so because we will lack the resources to see that Jesus challenges the family. On the contrary, we have been led to believe that Christianity is good for the nation because Christianity is good for the family. We therefore fail to stand under the authority of the Word because the Word is captured by practices and narratives that are more constitutive of that entity called America than that community called Church. Indeed the confusions of those narratives have made it impossible for us to rightly be proclaimers and hearers of the Word.

In like manner, many of these sermons deal with non-violence. The Church's acceptance of war as a necessary feature of Christian life makes it impossible for us to hear the Sermon on the Mount as people who are, or who compose, the Church. Therefore the "Sermon on the Sermon on the Mount" is an attempt to help us see how the practice of reconciliation is a crucial political practice for rightly hearing and living the sermon. Many of these sermons deal with reconciliation as a political process in order to help us see the contrast to the politics built on envy and resentment. In particular, the sermon on Thomas, which was preached the Sunday after Easter when we are asked by the Church to remember the Holocaust, is I think, the most troubling account of what such a politics might look like.

The sermons are arranged in an order I find useful, but they are not meant to build one on the other. They are occasional. Many were preached to seminarians in York Chapel at Duke Divinity School. I hope that they share in common what an extraordinary thing it is to preach from the Bible when it is assumed that the discourse makes no sense apart from a people constituted as Church. In that context we can preach and hear as those that rightly stand under the authority of the Word.[10] That does not mean that every sermon has the authority of the Church, but rather it means that insofar as it is the Word of God, it is by necessity the Word of the whole Church. Sermons, when preached with authority, thus become one of our most important resources for capturing the Bible from the politics of America. May we learn to preach and hear with the courage instilled by the Spirit of God.

PART TWO

THE POLITICS OF SCRIPTURE:
Sermonic Exhibits

Before reading the following sermons, it is necessary to read the scriptures appointed. Part of the practice is the interaction between your reading and my sermons.

5

The Insufficiency of Scripture:

Why Discipleship Is Required

Isaiah 25:6-9
Luke 24:13-35

My family loves to tell the story of my cousin Billy Dick. The very name, Billy Dick, indicates that we are Texans. One Easter, when Billy Dick was six, he was in Sunday school at Lakewood Methodist Church in Dallas, Texas. He was listening to the story of the crucifixion. He suddenly realized that the crucifixion was a very unhappy affair. He waved his hand in a desperate attempt to attract the teacher's attention. The teacher finally acknowledged him. He stood up and blurted out, "If Roy Rogers had been there, those dirty S.O.B.s would not have been able to do it!"

My family loves this story even though the language is a bit embarrassing. The language, after all, is familiar—coming, as we do, from the world of bricklaying. We like the story also because it underwrites a sense of who we are. We do not think of ourselves as among the makers and breakers of a society but rather as the kind of simple people who do the right thing, year after year. Such modesty, however, can hide very strong moral idealism. For we believe that if we had been at the crucifixion we certainly would not have let it happen. We are not the kind of people who let inno-cent people be killed.

We would rescue a savior who dies with the blazing guns of Roy Rogers

Yet my family tends to miss the irony of Billy Dick's story. For that story presumes that we would rescue a savior who dies with the blazing six-guns of Roy Rogers. We assume that there is no inherent incompatibility between our use of violence and what Jesus was about.

I think my family in that regard is no different from most Christians today. We believe that, on the whole, we should be nonviolent except when there is a real crisis. I often ask my students, for example, if it might be a good idea to keep a gun in church. After all, many of them serve in the mountains of western Carolina, and you never know when a motorcycle gang might break into the church, threatening to rape the women and make the men watch. So the idea that we ought to keep a gun rack under the Cross, preferably with a sub-machine gun in it, seems quite sensible. They are rather taken aback at that suggestion, but I suspect that most of us harbor the assumption that there must be guns in our lives if for no other reason than we never know when we might be asked to defend the innocent.

Not only my family but most of us like Billy Dick's appeal to Roy Rogers. We might say it differently, with much more sophistication, but we do not believe that we would have let Jesus be unjustly crucified. Part of the appeal of Billy Dick's reaction to the crucifixion is, of course, the general American penchant for siding with the underdog. We entertain imaginatively heroic roles, assuming when the time comes that we will be ready to rise to the occasion. We assume if we had just been there with Jesus, if we had just been able to follow him day in and day out—to witness his miracles, to hear his teachings, to observe his confrontations with the leaders of the society—we would have been faithful. We would not have abandoned him at the Cross. We are even more confident that we would have recognized him if Jesus had joined us on the road to Emmaus.

That we think we would have stood with Jesus against the crucifixion, that we think that we would recognize him after the resurrection are extraordinary presumptions. Just to the extent that we find our lives embedded in the gospel it makes clear that most of us, even if we had known all there was to know about Jesus, would have been, at worst, in the crowd shouting "Crucify him, crucify him!" At best, we would have returned to Galilee thinking it was good while it lasted, but we had better get back to the "real world." If I had missed being there to shout "Crucify him, crucify him," I am sure it would not have been because I sided with Jesus but rather because of my dislike of crowds.

To claim that if Jesus had joined us on the Emmaus road, we would have recognized him is not unlike claiming that in order to understand the Scripture all we have to do is pick it up and read it. Both claims assume that "the facts are just there" and that reasonable people are able to see the facts if their minds are not clouded. Yet as we shall see, the story of the Emmaus road makes clear that knowing the Scripture does little good unless we know it as part of a people constituted by the practices of a resurrected Lord. So Scripture will not be self-interpreting or plain in its meaning unless we have been transformed in order to be capable of reading it.

The story of the Emmaus road neatly challenges our

presumption that a resurrected Lord would be readily recognizable. We are simply told that "two of them" were leaving Jerusalem, walking toward Emmaus, discussing what had happened over the past few days. It seems that they must have seen, for example, a cleansing of the Temple or perhaps observed the examination of Jesus before the Sanhedrin. Perhaps these people may well have been following Jesus for some time, having heard the Sermon on the Mount or having observed his miracles. They seem to be close associates of Jesus, not perhaps among the apostles, but nonetheless people deeply attracted to what Jesus was about.

I tend to think of these two as admirers. I do so because they remind me of a story that Jim McClendon reports about Clarence Jordan. Clarence Jordan was the founder of the Koinonia Farm near Americus, Georgia. It was set up to be an interracial community before anyone knew what civil rights were all about. Jordan himself was a pacifist as well as an integrationist and thus was not a popular figure in Georgia, even though he came from a prominent family.

The Koinonia Farm, by its very nature, was controversial and, of course, it was in trouble. McClendon reports that in the early fifties Clarence approached his brother Robert Jordan (later a state senator and justice of the Georgia Supreme Court) to ask him to legally represent the Koinonia Farm. Robert responded to Clarence's request:

"Clarence, I can't do that. You know my political aspirations. Why, if I represented you, I might lose my job, my house, everything I've got."

"*We* might lose everything too, Bob."

"It's different for you."

"Why is it different? I remember, it seems to me, that you and I joined the church the same Sunday, as boys. I expect when we came forward the preacher asked me about the same question he did you. He asked me, 'Do you accept Jesus as your Lord and Savior.' And I said, 'Yes.' What did you say?"

"I follow Jesus, Clarence, up to a point."

"Could that point by any chance be—the cross?"

"That's right. I follow him to the cross, but not *on* the cross. I'm not getting myself crucified."

"Then I don't believe you're a disciple. You're an admirer of Jesus, but not a disciple of his. I think you ought to go back to the church you belong to, and tell them you're an admirer not a disciple."

"Well now, if everyone who felt like I do did that, we wouldn't *have* a church, would we?"

"The question," Clarence said, "is, Do you have a church?"[1]

That we find these two on the way to Emmaus, walking away from Jerusalem, gives us some basis for thinking that they were admirers not unlike Robert Jordan. They clearly understood that what had been taking place in Jerusalem around this man Jesus concerned very serious matters indeed. In fact, they were continuing to discuss it in an effort to understand what had taken place. Maybe they were not admirers. Perhaps they were intellectuals or even theologians. One can almost hear them say, "That was really an interesting set of suggestions Jesus had to make about the kingdom. Damned insight-

Perhaps they were intellectuals or even theologians. One can almost hear them say, "That was really an interesting set of suggestions Jesus had to make about the kingdom. Damned insightful, though a bit overstated I must say."

ful, though a bit overstated I must say. Though he is quite provocative, he really lacks the characteristics of a carefully trained mind."

Because they are so enthralled with the events in Jerusalem around Jesus, they are astounded that this stranger who joins them on the way to Emmaus seems to know nothing about those events. He was coming from Jerusalem, and surely he must have known the front-page news of the day. Yet he has to ask them what they are talking about. It surely seems that this stranger is at a disadvantage.

However, as they proceed on their way to Emmaus, instructing Jesus along the way, it is remarkable that they do not recognize who he is. We tend to blame them for this, but perhaps we are far too quick. We are not talking "regular stuff" here. We are talking about the resurrection. Our expectation that these two on the way to Emmaus should recognize Jesus shows us how difficult it is for any of us to comprehend the resurrection. No matter how hard we try, it is difficult to shake the picture that the resurrection is the resuscitation of a corpse that we would recognize if confronted by it.

Of course that is exactly what the resurrection is not. It is not the resuscitation of a corpse but rather the final eschatological act by God through which the Kingdom stamp is put on this man Jesus as the decisive life for the inauguration of a new age. Resurrection is the reconfiguration of all we know, have known, and will know. It is that which forces a redescription of all history as well as the movement of the planets. Resurrection is Kingdom come in the person and work of this man Jesus. It is, to quote the wonderful title of Allen Verhey's book, "the great reversal."

That Jesus has been marked by such a stamp must surely make us think twice about our claim that we would be able to easily spot him—this man, this crucified Messiah—just as he is also the power that moves the sun and the stars. We do not readily comprehend that here in this cross and resurrection the very destiny of the cosmos is determined. It is surely presumptuous on our part that we would easily recognize him. We should be much more sympathetic to the two on the way to Emmaus than we were initially.

But if their failure to recognize Jesus is a reminder that the resurrection is not a resuscitated corpse, it also renders problematic all subjectivistic theories of the resurrection. Those theories suggest that Jesus' resurrection is merely a poetic, symbolic, or mythological way of describing the disciples' sense of the continuing presence of Jesus. Such accounts of the resurrection are compared to memories of outstanding figures such as Gandhi, Martin Luther King, Jr., or Dorothy Day. We tend to imagine the resurrection in these terms as if we were friends sharing a meal, discussing all that Jesus had done, and suddenly thinking that the very experience of discussing Jesus made Jesus still alive. Such theories assume that the experience we have is itself the resurrection. We fail to understand that God's resurrection of Jesus is not defined by what we may or may not experience.

> *We tend to imagine the resurrection . . . as if we were friends sharing a meal, discussing all that Jesus had done, and suddenly thinking that the very experience of discussing Jesus made Jesus still alive.*

One of the problems with such subjectivistic accounts of the resurrection is that they make the resurrected Jesus far too familiar, far too subject to our needs and wants. Indeed, it makes us lose the eschatological character of the resurrection entirely, as we force Jesus into the limits of our lives. In fact, the resurrection forces our lives to conform to God's kingdom. The early Christians' discovery that they could pray to Jesus, that they could worship Jesus, is intelligible only if this Jesus is the resurrected Lord of all creation.

Therefore, that these two admirers of Jesus did not recognize him is a reminder to us that Jesus, after the resurrection, is a stranger. We cannot recognize him by looking, but we have to be instructed through the lives of others. We must learn that, resurrected though he may be, it is the crucified Jesus that is so resurrected. Jesus is not the exemplification of savior stories that we have learned elsewhere, but he is the defining figure for what salvation means. That is why Hans Frei, in his *Identity of Jesus Christ,* rightly reminds us that Jesus is no Christ figure since he was the Christ. He was not a "man for others," for there have been many such people. Rather, this Jesus is the eschatological Messiah of the God of Israel who makes possible the calling of the Church into existence, so that the world might know that our destiny is determined by a Kingdom that the world cannot know apart from this man. Therefore, in order to recognize this Messiah, this crucified but risen Jesus, we need training and instruction. We do not possess in ourselves what we need to recognize Jesus as the resurrected Lord because such recognition depends upon training by that very Lord. That such training is required is clear from the way Jesus' companions try to explain why they are leaving Jerusalem. In their explanations it is clear that they do not recognize this companion as the resurrected Jesus for the simple reason that they have not understood the Jesus of Golgotha.

They had thought that in this man Jesus they had found the long-expected Messiah. They acknowledge that Jesus was no doubt a powerful prophet in word and deed. In fact they thought he had the potential to set Israel free. "But we had hoped that he was the one to redeem Israel." The redemption of Israel is after all the political freeing of the people of Israel from perpetual control of others. It is the rebirth of the land of Palestine. They were sure that this Jesus had the power to effect this.

Yet they say that the leaders conspired to kill him, and they accomplished their task well. They had seen the crucifixion it seems. Even more they had now heard that the tomb was empty. The women say it is empty. The women and others even saw an angel who said that Jesus was alive. They acknowledged that some have verified all this. Jesus is not in the grave. He is not there. It is not clear where he is.

Now you must wonder about our companions on the way to Emmaus at this point. If the tomb is empty, and this has been verified, why are they leaving Jerusalem? You would think that they might want to stay around and find out what has happened. While there have certainly been people raised from the dead in the past, you would think that it is a fairly extraordinary event and that they would have wanted to stay around to find out what had happened. But no, they leave Jerusalem thinking that they had seen all that they had needed to see. They start to Emmaus.

How can we explain this strange behavior? Surely even if Jesus is alive, even if Jesus is resurrected, they wanted a different outcome. He is not, it seems, the Messiah who was to liberate Israel. What does resurrection have to do with the liberation of Israel? Resurrection is not the politics for which they had looked. So they could not see the resurrected Jesus because the resurrected Jesus embodied the politics of a Kingdom for which they were unprepared.

Jesus therefore has to begin to explain to them what they had seen in Jerusalem. He points out to them that

> *This is not a death that is sacrificial in and of itself, but rather it is a death required by the very politics of the Kingdom.*

they had missed the very meaning of the prophets who had taught them that "the Messiah had to undergo much to enter into his glory." And Jesus must begin with Moses to show them the kind of Messiah that was among them—namely, a Messiah whose politics required that he be killed in order that the world might know the character of God's kingdom. This is not a death that is sacrificial in and of itself, but rather it is a death required by the very politics of the Kingdom. For Jesus has come that some of us might be called from the world—which had not yet been made until Jesus came—that we may live in a manner different from the violence of the world.

As Jesus explained the Scripture, we have what might be called a hermeneutical moment. But it is not just explaining the text and what it meant that Jesus is about, for these people on the way to Emmaus clearly seemed to have known the text. Their problem was that they did not know how to find Jesus in it. They had not received the training that would instill in them a whole set of practices that would give the text a whole different reading.

In effect, Jesus had to deconstruct their narratives so that they might see, for example, why a text such as Isaiah 52 and 53 is about Jesus.

Isaiah 52:13-15

See, my servant shall prosper;
  he shall be exalted and
    lifted up,
  and shall be very high.
Just as there were many who

were astonished at him
—so marred was his
  appearance, beyond
  human semblance,
and his form beyond that of
  mortals—
so he shall startle many nations;

kings shall shut their mouths
because of him;
for that which had not been
told them they shall see,
and that which they had not
heard they shall
contemplate.

Isaiah 53:3, 5-12

He was despised and rejected
by others;
a man of suffering and
acquainted with infirmity;
and as one from whom others
hide their faces
he was despised, and we
held him of no account.
But he was wounded for our
transgressions,
crushed for our iniquities;
upon him was the punishment
that made us whole,
and by his bruises we are
healed.
All we like sheep have gone
astray;
we have all turned to our
own way,
and the LORD has laid on him
the iniquity of us all.

He was oppressed, and he was
afflicted,
yet he did not open his
mouth;
like a lamb that is led to the
slaughter,
and like a sheep that before
its shearers is silent,
so he did not open his
mouth.
By a perversion of justice he
was taken away.
Who could have imagined
his future?
For he was cut off from the
land of the living,
stricken for the transgression
of my people.
They made his grave with the
wicked
and his tomb with the rich,
although he had done no
violence,
and there was no deceit in
his mouth.

Yet it was the will of the LORD
to crush him with pain.
When you make his life an
offering for sin,
he shall see his offspring,
and shall prolong his days;
through him the will of the
LORD shall prosper.
Out of his anguish he shall
see light;
he shall find satisfaction
through his knowledge.
The righteous one, my
servant, shall make many
righteous,
and he shall bear their
iniquities.
Therefore I will allot him a

portion with the great,
and he shall divide the spoil
with the strong;
because he poured out
himself to death,

and was numbered with
the transgressors;
yet he bore the sin of many,
and made intercession
for the trangressors.

We assume under the authority of the Church that when we hear these texts from Isaiah that they are about Jesus. We can assume that because we are on this side of Emmaus. We have become trained in this kind of rereading, but our companions on the way to Emmaus did not assume that these texts were about Jesus. They had to be taught that such texts are about Jesus by Jesus. I am sure, moreover, that as their companions we must continue to relearn this over and over again.

We never learn this lesson well because we and our companions on the way to Emmaus assume that Messiahs are people of power, not suffering servants such as we find in Isaiah. Søren Kierkegaard tells a story, which I retell, that exemplifies our presumptions about these matters. It is a story about a prince and beautiful peasant maiden. The prince spots this beautiful young woman one day when he is riding in his fields. She is gathering wheat. Watching her work he falls deeply in love, but vows to win her without using his power as prince. So he returns to his castle, puts on peasant clothes over the purple, and goes to work beside her.

Kierkegaard observes that our attention is held in this story not by whether this beautiful peasant young woman will come to love the prince. He is, after all, a noble and handsome prince. They are both young, and there is no doubt that they will love each other. Rather our attention is grabbed in such a story by predicting—when will he tell her he is the prince? Will it be perhaps at a break in their work, after she has come to know him over weeks and months? During that break he will declare his love, and she, perhaps demurely, will respond positively? With that response, will he rip back the coarse cloth of the peasant and reveal the purple underneath?

Storytellers, of course, are wonderful in how they build our suspense. Perhaps he will wait until the wedding. After she pledges her troth, and he does likewise, then he will rip back the peasant clothes and reveal the purple. Perhaps he will even wait until after the wedding, when he will say, "You have not only become my wife, but indeed you are the princess of the land." Such a story is romantic, and it rightly holds our attention. Kierkegaard notes that ironically such stories also determine how we think of Jesus. For we tend to think that Jesus is like a prince pretending to have coarse cloth of the human—of crucifixion, of death, of powerlessness—that covers the purple. There really is the kind of power here that the world knows. We must wait for him to rip it away so the purple will be revealed. That rip we think to be the resurrection. There is the purple that makes it possible for Christians to acquire the power to rule the world. That is the politics we want through this Jesus.

Yet in Jesus there is no purple other than the crucifixion—the purple is the blood of the cross. There is no hidden power here. For our savior comes not as the world knows power figures. Rather our savior comes offering us the practice of reconciliation necessary for us to be a people capable of living, without violence or envy, in the world. Like our counterparts on the way to Emmaus, we expected a politics of power from this Messiah, and instead we get crucifixion and resurrection. Like our companions on the way to Emmaus, we want the certainty and power of a text, but instead we get the call to discipleship. So like those on the way to Emmaus, who now have the disadvantage of enjoying an account of Christianity that we believe puts us in control of history, we continue to fail to recognize this One who comes to call those able to live without control.

Yet after Jesus' explication of the Scriptures, we see that

our companions on the road to Emmaus still cannot see who it is that has joined them. Nonetheless, in general they have found it pleasant to be with him. So, even though he seems bent on going farther, they suggest he spend the night with them. As they sit together, as he breaks the bread, their eyes are opened and they recognize him. The guest had become the host, reconstituting the very meaning of hospitality.

But upon recognition he disappears. Their eyes have been opened. Adam's and Eve's eyes were opened, and they were blind. Now, through the sharing of Christ's presence in the meal, our blindness is reversed and we see. The effects of sin are turned back, and we are made new creatures capable of being in communion with one another through Christ.

Once you have such a presence, you no longer need an appearance.

What are we to make of this strange occurrence? Certainly it at least means that Jesus is present to the disciples on the way to Emmaus and to us most powerfully in the fellowship meal of the new age in which he has made it possible for us to share. Surely this must mean that the presence we have with Christ at Eucharist is even more determinative than an appearance on the way to Emmaus. Once you have such a presence, you no longer need an appearance.

Indeed one suspects that part of the felt need for something as absurd as "the search for the historical Jesus" may have some connection with the fact that these guests tend to originate in those traditions where Eucharist is celebrated not as presence but rather as absence. The search for the historical Jesus is a substitute for the willingness to share the life of Christ. It presumes that if we could just get the facts right, we could really make up our minds about whether our life could be fully shaped by the Kingdom, which is determined by this man's life. Yet the "real historical Jesus" or the "objective text of Scripture" cannot be substituted for the reality of Christ that is found through the sharing of this meal.

In receiving food from Jesus after Easter we receive the gift of his life, God's life, through which we are made part of the adventure called Kingdom. Through the sharing of God's very life as Trinity we are made part of a community that can live by forgiveness rather than by hate, envy, and resentment. It is a community that is the creation of a new time and a new age. That is why all readings from the past must be transformed by the habits of this community. In this meal we learn of God's unfailing hospitality, of God's unrelenting desire to be reconciled to us, thus making it possible for us to be a community of peace in a violent world.

Jesus' cross and resurrection are not just exchanges between himself and God. God is not playing games with himself, but rather Jesus' resurrection makes us agents in God's history of reconciliation by transforming us into a community of the reconciled. The good news is that we were once no people, but now we are a people of peace that stand as a sign that resurrection is the end of the new beginning for the world. The reality of the resurrection is thus manifest in the fact that we exist. We exist as a people who testify in the resurrection of this man that God has destroyed, as was promised in Isaiah:

> The shroud that is cast over all the peoples,
> the sheet that is spread over all nations;
> he will swallow up death forever. (Isaiah 25:7)

Christ has become our temple through which all are now directed to worship that all creation may be made at one and at peace with God.

So as we again and again are welcomed by this host at his meal of the kingdom of peace, we become people of peace and reconciliation. Only such a people are capable of recognizing and witnessing to others concerning this stranger who is the heart of our existence. Only such a people will be capable of rightly reading the Scripture. Only such a people are capable of in fact performing the Scripture.

In *Christianity Rediscovered,* Vincent Donovan tells of his mission work with the Masai. One of the most significant gestures for the Masai is to offer one another a handful of grass as a sign of peace, happiness, and well-being. During arguments that might arise, a tuft of grass offered by one Masai and accepted by another is an assurance that no violence will erupt because of the argument. As Donovan says, "No Masai would violate that sacred sign of peace offered, because it was not only a sign of peace; it was peace."[2]

Donovan describes how the Mass begins among the Masai as soon as the priest enters the village. Dancing begins as well as praying for the sick. This can last for a whole day before the climax in eucharistic celebration. Yet he says he never knew if Eucharist would in fact emerge from all this. For the leaders of the village would be the ones to decide if the Eucharist was to be performed. For if the life in the village had been less than holy, then there was no Mass. If there had been selfishness and forgetfulness and hatefulness and lack of forgiveness in the work and life of the community, they would not make a sacrilege out of the Eucharist by calling it the Body of Christ. Donovan says that from time to time leaders did decide, despite the prayers and readings and discussions, there would be no Eucharist.

So when we wish for the peace of Christ for one another, let us remember it is by this wishing that we are able to recognize the presence of this stranger, our resurrected Lord, and in that recognition lies our salvation. The resurrected Lord is a stranger, but he is also the host that invites us to become his friend and thus become friends with ourselves and others; so let us keep the feast of peace and reconciliation made possible because our Lord has risen from the grave. Perhaps even the world will see that we are a "biblical people."

6

A Sermon on the Sermon on the Mount

A Modest Proposal for Peace: Let the Christians of the World Agree That They Will Not Kill One Another

So reads the poster and postcards distributed by the Mennonite Central Committee. I have the poster on my office door at the Divinity School. Occasionally I have notes slipped under my door that say, "How dare you—why should Christians only refrain from killing other Christians? This is just another example of Christian self-centeredness." Sometimes someone will even knock and challenge me with the same sort of statements. My response is always the same: "I agree that it would certainly be a good thing for Christians to stop killing anyone, but you have to start somewhere."

That is why this statement is a modest proposal. Just think, for example, if we had taken it seriously in Iraq. There are many Christians in Iraq. Could Christians who flew the bombers have accomplished their missions as readily if they had to think about where the Christians in Iraq were living?

However, before we get too involved with these questions I need to say why I begin with the Mennonite proposal when I am supposed to be preaching on the Sermon on the Mount. I do so because I want to maintain that unless we are a people formed by a practice suggested by the proposal, we lack the resources properly to understand, much less live, the Sermon—which, by the way, ought to be the same thing.

In short, I maintain that the Sermon on the Mount presupposes the existence of a community constituted by the practice of nonviolence, and it is unintelligible divorced from such a community. Or, put as contentiously as I can, you cannot rightly read the Sermon on the Mount unless you are a pacifist. I

> *You cannot rightly read the Sermon on the Mount unless you are a pacifist.*

know that sounds threatening to many of you who think of yourselves as generally nonviolent but with exceptions—defense of family, nation, and so on. I assume that means you are already a pacifist and we are just in an argument about exceptions, because you assume that users of violence bear the burden of proof. "Just war" theory is in this sense a theory of exception for testing the small range of cases when violence might be tragically necessary.

By raising the issue of pacifism I mean to suggest quite a different set of considerations. For example, I call myself a pacifist in public because I am obviously so violent. Hopefully by creating expectations in you about me, you will help keep me faithful to what I know is true. In like manner I want to suggest that the Sermon on the Mount constitutes and is constituted by a community that has learned that to live in the manner described in the Sermon requires learning to trust in others to help me so live. In other words, the object of the Sermon on the Mount is to create dependence; it is to force us to need one another.

This means that the Sermon on the Mount obviously

makes no sense to those not formed into that body called Church. This is particularly the case in our society when we are told that to be human means to be independent, to be able to take care of ourselves. So to interpret the Sermon on the Mount properly means we must already be a people who are formed by community habits that those who do not worship Jesus cannot be expected to have.

This way of approaching the Sermon is, of course, quite different from many of the approaches to the Sermon in Christian tradition. Those approaches are generally about helping us see why the Sermon is not meant to be taken literally. For example, some have said that the demands of the Sermon, particularly those associated with "You have heard . . . but I say to you . . ." are only for the select few—the religious, the celibate, and so on. But there is no indication that Jesus so limited what he was saying. Accepting this limited application results in a two-tiered ethics that defies our understanding that the whole Church is called to be holy.

A more common interpretation is that the Sermon is a law that presents an impossibly high ideal to drive us to a recognition of our sin. It is meant to drive us to grace. In other words, it is not really meant to tell us what to do, but rather to remind us that Christian moral life is about love. This view makes the Christian life so interior that Christians are to do whatever we do from the motive of love. "Love and do what you will." Bad advice if I have ever heard it! It has an even worse effect on Christology. Why would anyone ever have put Jesus to death if it is all just a matter of being loving?

Indeed when we approach the Sermon primarily with an attitude—"Do we have to take this literally?"—we lose sight of the fact that this is a sermon preached by Jesus. It makes all the difference who is the proclaimer—namely Jesus, the Jesus who proclaimed the inauguration of a new age. He does not merely proclaim it; he is the inauguration of that age. The message of the Sermon cannot be separated, abstracted out, from the messenger. If Jesus is the eschatological messiah, then he has made it possible through his death and resurrection for us to live in accordance with the life envisioned in the Sermon. The Sermon is but the form of his life, and his life is the prism through which the Sermon is refracted. In short, the Sermon does not appear impossible to a people who have been called to a life of discipleship, which requires them to contemplate their death in the light of the cross.

Gene Davenport, in his book on the Sermon on the Mount, *Into the Darkness,* reminds us that "when the first hearers of Matthew's Gospel heard Jesus' call to suffer rather than to inflict suffering, to accept death rather than to inflict death, to reject all efforts to save themselves from their plight by military action and to leave their deliverance to God, they knew that the one who gave such scandalous instruction had himself lived and died in accord with that call. The Jesus of the Sermon on the Mount is not one who extols an esoteric or naive or idealistic ethic—a way of life never tested or tried—but is one whose instruction sets forth the way of life which he himself embodied, the way of life that manifests God's own life."[1]

The Sermon was, as Davenport's exposition makes clear, the wisdom of the New Age, the wisdom of Light, which undercuts the usual wisdom of a society. Jesus is not teaching an "interim ethic" but rather is providing a new ordering for his followers. Such an ordering provides the skills for survival for those whose lives reflect the New Age but who will continue to live amid the realities of the Old Age. Their lives accordingly manifest the reality of the Light of the New Age but also illumine the darkness in which they must live.

Situated eschatologically, the question of whether the Sermon is meant to be "taken literally" loses its power. The Sermon is the constitution of God's Kingdom people for their journey between the ages. They are a people who have learned to live without vengeance, seeing as they do that revenge is darkness. As Davenport observes, "The oppressed who show mercy on their oppressors do not know what effect their mercy will have. The result may be martyrdom. The Reign of God is still a hidden reign. On the other hand, because God still opens the eyes of the blind, the result may be conversion. Either result holds out the possibility that at least some people, seeing, will recognize the good works and glorify God."[2]

Which brings us back to the relevance of the Mennonite proposal. The Mennonites, like Calvinists, are often accused of being legalists because they assume that the Sermon is meant to be followed. Yet it is their contention that the Sermon is not a "law-like" code to be applied caustically, but rather it is a description of the virtues of a community that embodies the peace that Christ has made possible among those who have been baptized into his death and resurrection. For example they assume that the Sermon works in a community determined by Matthew 18:15-22, in relation to fault:

> "If another member of the church sins against you, go and point out the fault when the two of you are alone. If the member listens to you, you have regained that one. But if you are not listened to, take one or two others along with you, so that every word may be confirmed by the evidence of two or three witnesses. If the member refuses to listen to them, tell it to the church; and if the offender refuses to listen even to the church, let such a one be to you as a Gentile and a tax collector. Truly I tell you, whatever you bind on earth will be bound in heaven, and whatever you loose on earth will be loosed in heaven. Again, truly I tell you, if

two of you agree on earth about anything you ask, it will be done for you by my Father in heaven. For where two or three are gathered in my name, I am there among them."

Then Peter came and said to him, "Lord, if another member of the church sins against me, how often should I forgive? As many as seven times?" Jesus said to him, "Not seven times, but, I tell you, seventy-seven times."

In other words, the Mennonites assume that the Sermon only makes sense in the context of a people committed to the process necessary for reconciliation to one another. This is a body of people who have been trained to be forgiven. When we hear these passages we always think of ourselves as the forgiver. But remember that the Christian community is constituted by the forgiven. Only communities of people so formed are capable of supporting one another in the demanding task of forgiving the enemy—who too often turns out to be ourselves.

"You are accepted," "I'm okay, you're okay" may be good pop theology or psychology—though I doubt it—but it is not the gritty reality of actual reconciliation that is characteristic of Christian repentance.

Moreover it must be remembered that such forgiveness is a *practice* of reconciliation. "You are accepted" or "I'm okay, you're okay" may be good pop theology or psychology—though I doubt it—but it is not the gritty reality of actual reconciliation that is characteristic of Christian repentance. As the awkward Reverend Emmett, of the Church of the Second Chance in Anne Tyler's novel *Saint Maybe,* tells Ian Bledsoe, who has asked to be forgiven for contributing to the possible suicide of his brother, "You can't just say, 'I'm sorry, God.'

Why anyone could do that much! You have to offer reparation—concrete, practical reparation, according to the rules of our church."³

Ian resists but submits by dropping out of college, taking responsibility for his brother's three orphaned children, and becoming a member of the Church of the Second Chance. His brother's death cannot be undone, but in the practice of living a reconciled life with others he discovers that he is made more than he otherwise would be. Forgiveness and reconciliation name the practice through which the Church acquires a history that makes it God's alternative to the hatred of both self and other, which is fueled by our fear of the acknowledgment of our sin.

When the Sermon is divorced from such ecclesial contexts, it cannot help appearing as an abstract law that comes from nowhere and is to be applied to equally anonymous individuals. But that is contrary to the fundamental presupposition of the Sermon, which is that individuals divorced from this community of the New Age made possible by Christ are, of course, incapable of living the life that the Sermon depicts. All the so-called hard sayings of the Sermon are designed to remind us that we cannot live without depending on the support and trust of others. We are told not to lay up treasure for ourselves, so we must learn to share. We are told not to be anxious, not to try to ensure our future, thus making it necessary to rely on one another for our food, our clothing, and our housing. We are told not to judge, thereby requiring that we live honestly and truthfully with one another. Such a people have no need to parade their piety because they know that in a fundamental sense it is not theirs. Rather, the piety of the community capable of hearing and living by the Sermon is a gift that God gives them through making them learn to serve one another. Such a piety exceeds that of the scribes and Pharisees.

Surely this is also the necessary presupposition for understanding the antitheses in chapter 5 of Matthew. To be capable of living chastely, to marry without recourse to divorce, to live without the necessity of oaths, to refrain from returning evil with evil, to learn to love the enemy— all of these are surely impossible for isolated individuals. As individuals we can no more act in these ways than we can force our wills not to be anxious, for the very attempt to will not to be anxious only creates anxiety. Freedom from anxiety is possible only when we are part of a community that is constituted by such a compelling adventure that we forget our fears in the joy of the New Age. As Richard Lischer explains, "The Sermon portrays a dynamic constellation of relationships—a kind of radical-ized Canterbury Tales—within the pilgrim community. Because the pilgrims have experienced by faith the assur-ance of their destination, they are encouraged by its promise and guided by its rubrics."[4]

The attempt to turn the Sermon into an ethic abstracted from the eschatological community cannot help breeding self-righteousness and ultimately making the gospel appear ridiculous. As Lischer puts it:

> Our only hope of living as the community of the Sermon is to acknowledge that we do not retaliate, hate, curse, lust, divorce, swear, brag, preen, worry, or backbite because it is not in the nature of our God or our destination that we should be such people. When we as individuals fail in these instances, we do not snatch up cheap forgiveness, but we do remember that the ecclesial is larger than the sum of our individual failures and that it is pointed in a direction that will carry us away from them.[5]

The Sermon's ecclesial presuppositions are nowhere more clearly confirmed than in the Beatitudes. There we see that the gospel is the proclamation of a new set of relations made possible by a people being drawn into a new movement. The temptation is to read the Beatitudes as a list of virtues that good people ought to have or as deeds they ought to do. We thus think we ought to try to be meek, or poor, or hungry, or merciful, or peacemakers, or persecuted. Yet we know that it is hard to try to be meek—either you are meek or you are not. Even more difficult is it to have all the characteristics of the Beatitudes at once!

Yet that is not what it means to be blessed. Rather the Beatitudes assume that there are already people in the community who find themselves in these postures. To be blessed does not mean "if you are this way you will be rewarded," but that "happy are they who find they are so constituted within the community." Moreover, the Beatitudes assume that we are part of a community with diversity of gifts—a diversity that creates not envy but cooperation and love.

It is only against a background like this that we can begin to understand the illegitimacy of questions such as, Does the Sermon on the Mount require me to be a pacifist? The Christians who remembered the Sermon did not know they were pacifists. Rather, they knew as a community they were part of a new way of resolving disputes—through confrontation, forgiveness, and reconciliation. Peacemaking is not an abstract principle but rather the practice of a community made possible by the life, death, and resurrection of Jesus.

There is nothing optimistic about such a practice. The Sermon does not promise that if we merely love our enemies, they will no longer be our enemies. The Sermon does not promise that if we turn our right cheek, we will not be hit again. The Sermon does not promise that if we simply act in accordance with its dictates, the world will be free of war. But the Christian does not renounce war because one can expect intelligent citizens to rally around. They usually will not. The believer takes that stand because the defenseless death of the Messiah has, for all time, been revealed as the victory of faith that overcomes the world.

The Sermon does not generate an ethic of nonviolence, but rather a community of nonviolence is necessary if the Sermon is to be read rightly. Without such a community, the world has no way of knowing that all God's creation was meant to live in peace. There is, therefore, nothing more important that we can do for the world as Christians than to resolve not to kill one another. When we so live, the world will be able to see the Sermon on the Mount not as just another example of repressive law, but as gospel. In short, as Christians we will be called blessed if we live as a people of nonviolence.

CHAPTER 7

You Are Not Accepted

Isaiah 25:1-9
Philippians 4:4-13
Matthew 22:1-14

Do we not know what it means to be struck by grace? It does not mean that we suddenly believe that God exists, or that Jesus is the Savior, or that the Bible contains truth. To believe that something is, is almost contrary to the meaning of grace. Furthermore, grace does not mean simply that we are making progress in our moral self-control, in our fight against special faults, in our relationship to men and society. Moral progress may be a fruit of grace; but it is not grace itself, and it can even prevent us from receiving grace. For there is too often a graceless acceptance of Christian doctrine and a graceless battle against the structures of evil in our personalities. Such a graceless relation to God may lead us by necessity either to arrogance or to despair. It would be better to refuse God and the Christ and the Bible than to accept them without grace. For if we accept without grace, we do so in a state of separation, and can only succeed in deepening the separation. We cannot transform our lives, unless we allow them to be transformed by that stroke of grace. It happens; or it does not happen. And certainly it does not happen if we try to force it upon ourselves, just as it shall not happen so long as we think, in our self complacency, that we have no need of it. Grace strikes us when we are in great pain and restlessness. It strikes us when we walk through the dark valley of meaninglessness and empty life. It strikes us when we feel that our separation is deeper than usual, because we have violated another life, a life which we loved, or from which we were estranged. It strikes us when our disgust for our own being, our indifference, our weakness, our hostility, and our lack of direction and composure have become intolerable to us. It strikes us when, year after year, the longed for perfection of life does not appear, and the old compulsions reign within us as they have for decades, when despair destroys all joy and courage. Sometimes at that moment a wave of light breaks into our darkness and it is as though a voice saying: "You are accepted. You are accepted, accepted by that which is greater than you, in the name of which you do not know. Do not ask for that name now; perhaps you will find it later. Do not try to do anything now; perhaps later you will do much. Do not seek for anything; do not perform anything; do not intend anything. Simply accept the fact that you are accepted!" If that happens to us, we experience grace. After such an experience we may not be better than before, and we may not believe more than before. But everything is transformed. In that moment, grace conquers sin, reconciliation bridges the gulf of estrangement. And nothing is demanded of this experience, no religious or moral or intellectual presupposition, nothing but acceptance.[1]

So rang the words of Paul Tillich in what is perhaps the most notable sermon of the past fifty years. It stirs us still. It was a word we needed and need. It was a word that denied not the seriousness of sin. Sin, as Tillich told us, was not this or that wrong act, but rather sin is the essential alienation of self from self. Sin is separation. Before sin is act, it is this state of separation, which is the very character of our existence. Yet *grace* is a more profound word than *sin;* for when sin and grace are bound together, grace is finally more determinative than sin. For grace is more than gifts; grace is more than the good things that we would do and receive; grace is the reunion of life with life.

Grace is the acceptance of that which is rejected. Grace, therefore, like sin, is an ontological possibility written into the very nature of our existence.

Therefore, though modern people might think that they can live without these words—these seemingly outmoded words of sin and grace—they cannot be discarded. They cannot be replaced, for they are essential to indicating the reality in which we exist. Sin yes, but grace even more.

It has been one of the hallmarks of modern theology to be extraordinarily gracious about God's grace. There is

Every gasp and gulp is but a form of God's grace.

just nothing we can do to avoid being graced by God's grace. It's like the air we breathe, it's like the water we drink. Every gasp and gulp is but a form of God's grace. Accordingly, those who are associated with Christianity have consoled themselves with the fact that, even though fewer and fewer people count themselves Christian, no one can avoid God's grace. Thus we encounter the project of modern theology, which tries to show that atheism is fundamentally unintelligible. It is unintelligible not because all reality reflects the glory of the Father, Son, and Holy Spirit, but because as humans we are simply created in a fashion that invites us to accept our acceptance. Nature may be dumb to God's glory, but as humans our existential situation makes confrontation with the ground of our being unavoidable.

Against this background, the Gospel of Matthew makes jarring reading indeed. Jesus has entered Jerusalem triumphantly, riding on an ass. He drives the moneychangers from the Temple; his curse withers a fig tree; he confounds the chief priests and elders of the people about authority; he even suggests that it will be the whores and prostitutes who make it into the kingdom before these who would be righteous. Even more, in the parable of the wicked tenants we are told that God's kingdom will be given first to those who least expect it. In short, our text for today clearly appears in a context of conflict and judgment.

So Matthew continues:

> Once more Jesus spoke to them in parables, saying: "The kingdom of heaven may be compared to a king who gave a wedding banquet for his son. He sent his slaves to call those who had been invited to the wedding banquet, but they would not come. Again he sent other slaves, saying, 'Tell those who have been invited: Look, I prepared my dinner, my oxen and my fat calves have been slaughtered, and everything is ready; come to the wedding banquet.' But they made light of it and went away, one to his farm, another to his business, while the rest seized his slaves, mistreated them, and killed them. The king was enraged. He sent his troops, destroyed those murderers, and burned their city. Then he said to his slaves, 'The wedding is ready, but those invited were not worthy. Go therefore into the main streets, and invite everyone you find to the wedding banquet.' Those slaves went out into the streets and gathered all whom they found, both good and bad; so that the wedding hall was filled with guests.
>
> "But when the king came in to see the guests, he noticed a man there who was not wearing a wedding robe, and he said to him, 'Friend, how did you get in here without a wedding robe?' And he was speechless. Then the king said to the attendants, 'Bind him hand and foot, and throw him into the outer darkness, where there will be weeping and gnashing of teeth.' For many are called, but few are chosen." (Matt. 22:1-14)

What are we to do with a text like this in the light of our graciousness about God's grace? One of the ways we can

read it, of course, is to note that it really is not a text about
grace. Jesus is concerned in this parable about self-righteousness. Those who think that they have life by the tail—
who are in control, who have farms, who have businesses,
who think that they can take our representatives and kill
them—are people who are in trouble. Yet God's grace
comes to the outcast, to those who are not in control, to
those who are not so busy getting ahead that they can take
time to celebrate. It is the lowly who are, in fact, graced by
God's grace. It is the outcast person who has become worthy of being a wedding guest in our Lord's kingdom.

One of our favorite sermonic themes is that the poor
and the oppressed are the representatives of God's kingdom. That is surely what
this parable is about.
The irony of this theme, **This is about politics and**
of course, is that it **some are in and some are**
leaves most of us trying **out.**
to see if we can count
ourselves among the oppressed, among the victims. If we
are not victims, we fear we cannot be part of God's kingdom. Lacking clear signs of being oppressed, most of us
try to do the next best thing by claiming solidarity with the
poor and oppressed, so that we will show God that we
understand who embodies his kingdom and where the
kingdom is to be found.

But unfortunately our text really is not open to that
kind of construal. The king comes into the banquet hall
filled now with outcasts and people from the streets, and
lo and behold, he observes one there who is not dressed in
a wedding garment. A poor person, a street person, has
come to the wedding banquet as if it is not a banquet. And
the king says, "Friend, how did you even get in here without a wedding garment?" Apparently he makes no judgment yet, as he addresses him still as friend, but the man is

absolutely speechless. This lack of speech is decisive, for it shows that something more is at stake than simply being present, for we must be present and eager to be a celebrant. So this king, this seemingly gracious king, has the man bound hand and foot and thrown into outer darkness. The phrase "outer darkness," of course, is a way of reminding us that this is no ordinary banquet, but the banquet of God's new kingdom which is about our very destiny. So here we have one rejected. Here we have a sense that there is more to this "grace thing" than simply being accepted—namely, we are reminded, as we were told at the beginning of this text, that this is about God's kingdom. This is about politics and some are in and some are out. The question shifts: What is the condition of citizenship?

Of course we should have been prepared for this kind of judgment. Earlier in the text we are told that the king was enraged about the murder of his emissaries, so he had sent his troops and destroyed those murderers and burned their cities. Again we are not inclined to dwell on such matters. It just does not seem a gracious thing for a king to do, especially one who is preparing a wedding feast even for those who refuse to come to the wedding. We do not like to read texts, for example, like those in Isaiah where God is praised for turning the cities of our enemies into a heap, into a ruin, that will never be rebuilt. We like for God to aid the poor and the needy, but we are a little embarrassed when God seems so absolutely ruthless about such business. Defend the poor and the outcast, to be sure, but dear God, cannot you find a way to do it in a less bloody fashion? It is just not nice.

Which should make us reflect on why it is that we are concerned that God be so nice, so nonbloody? Might it not be that we know that we are rich, that we are those well off, and therefore we do not want God to be a God of vengeance? I suspect the reason why these passages, such as Isaiah 25, do not offend the poor is that they want God rightly to wreak havoc on the powerful. They do not want God to accept the oppressor; they want God to destroy the oppressor. They know that more is at stake in God's kingdom than simply accepting acceptance. They know that we are at war with powers who know nothing of a God that would rule the world from a cross. God's grace is not about acceptance; it is about judgment, it is about a kingdom that the world does not want. It is about a God who makes a difference, and that difference means that our lives must be transformed, or we will indeed be cast into outer darkness.

Of course, it may be objected that Tillich certainly understands that grace is about judgment. After all, Tillich was among those alleged "neo-orthodox" theologians who, in spite of their differences, shared a recovery of the significance of sin. It was Tillich in the same sermon that reminded us that our separation of life from life was seen most determinatively in the attitudes of social groups. Thus it is Tillich who can say:

> The madness of the German Nazis and the cruelty of the lynching mobs in the South provide too easy an excuse for us to turn our thoughts from our own selves. But let us just consider ourselves and what we feel, what we read, this morning and tonight, that in some sections of Europe all children under the age of three are sick and dying, or that in some section of Asia millions without homes are freezing and starving to death. The strangeness of life to life is evident in the strange fact that we can know all this, and yet can live today, this morning, tonight, as though we were completely ignorant. And I refer to the most sensitive people among us. In both mankind and nature, life is separated from life. Estrangement prevails among all things that live. Sins abound.[2]

Tillich obviously was not lacking in a sense of judgment. This is not the cheap grace that Bonhoeffer so effectively criticized. To be sure, there have been popularizations of Tillich that seem to suggest such cheapness. "You are accepted" can too easily become "I'm okay. You're okay." Yet there are surely ways to read Tillich, knowing well that we live in a world rightly deserving judgment.

> "You are accepted" can too easily become "I'm okay. You're okay."

It is not judgment that is missing from those who would proclaim the graciousness of God's grace, but missing is the mediator who is that grace. "You are accepted" is good Platonism, but it is not the grittiness of the gospel. *Grittiness* means that salvation for us in this world comes through the Jews. *Grittiness* means that the only way any of us will be part of God's celebration of the kingdom is through God's engrafting the Gentiles into that grace through Jesus of Nazareth. *Grittiness* means that salvation is now available to us through the people that Jesus made possible. The name we give these gritty people is Church.

We forget that we hear this text as Church. We are only here because our Christ has done battle with the powers that would rule our lives and has defeated them. It is a battle to which we continue to be called through being members of the Church. And Church is not incidental to that battle but essential for it. This is not a word we want to hear; it is not a word we want to hear in particular as Protestant Christians. We want to believe that being a member of the Church is but an incidental aspect of being saved. The Church is but the means that God uses to make the gospel known, which is open to anyone. We fear offending non-Christian brothers and sisters if we suggest to them that being a member of the Church might be part and parcel of what it means to be saved. We want our God to save us from the very notion that our salvation might depend upon there being a faithful body of people called out to be different from the world so that the world might know that God's salvation is as good as it is judgmental. Most of us are quite ready to acknowledge that the Church is important, but we all know it is just as sinful as any other institution; so let us always say to our nonchurched brothers and sisters that it is not necessary for them really to be part of us—you are accepted whether you know it or not.

Our refusal to take the Church seriously is, I suspect, the reason why so many of us find so bizarre actions like Richard Neuhaus leaving the Lutheran Church to become a Roman Catholic. It is not that he merely chose to become a Roman Catholic, but why would he have ever thought belonging to one church rather than another so important? It is important to be a member of the Church, but one church is probably just about as good as another. But of course that is exactly the reason Neuhaus became a Catholic. For it is Catholicism that continues to maintain that the Church is not incidental to God's providential care of the world, but necessary for that care.

Thus Neuhaus rightly says in his unpublished, but widely circulated, letter explaining his becoming a Catholic:

> The reformers rightly insisted that the Church lives from the Gospel and for the Gospel. Lutheranism, however, has not understood that the Church is an integral part of the Gospel. The Church is neither an abstract idea nor merely a voluntary association of believers, but a divinely commissioned and ordered community of apostolic faith, worship, and discipleship through time. "I delivered to you what I also received," said St. Paul (1 Corinthians 15), and of the guidance of the spirit promised the Church, apostolic scripture is joined to apostolic order in the faithful transmission and interpretation of revealed truth. The Gospel is

the proclamation of God's grace and Christ and his body the church. It is for the sake of the Gospel, and the unity of the Church gathered by that Gospel, that I am today a Roman Catholic.

Let us frankly say that most Protestants and many Roman Catholics do not believe that. We do not believe that the gospel is the proclamation of God's grace in Christ and the body of the Church. We generally want grace to be "You are accepted." We want grace to be an ontological possibility that we cannot avoid. We do not want grace mediated by a concrete historic people who embody the mediation of God's great good act for the world in the cross and resurrection of Jesus of Nazareth. God save us from that.

But that is the way God has saved us. Moreover, in that saving God has baptized us into the life and resurrection of Jesus so that we might be different people shining in the world that the world might know that God's kingdom is about a new age. It is a kingdom where people have been created to be gentle, as we are told in Philippians, even in a cruel world. That many will see such gentleness as judgment on cruelty is part of the witness. And they will want to kill us for our gentleness, but our gentleness is the way the world knows that God has called us to peace in a world at war. It is the way the world knows what it means for a community to be true, to be honorable, to be just, and even to be pure. Those are the ideals that make church Church. Those are the wedding garments that we have received in our baptism. Those are the clothes of righteousness that come from being made citizens of God's kingdom.

> *And they will want to kill us for our gentleness.*

Without such clothes, the news of our acceptance is not good news but bad news, for who wants to be accepted as we are? The good news is that by being made part of God's people through immersion in the fire and water of baptism, we are made anew. We can therefore come to God's celebratory meal, dressed in the wedding garments of our baptism, thus making clear to the world that so clothed, though we be poor and oppressed, the powers of this world cannot make us victims. With Christ we have been raised from the dead and clothed with the ideals of his kingdom and thus are no longer subject to the powers that pretend to rule this world. They are not accepted. Does that not sound like good news indeed? Amen.

8

On Having the Grace to Live Contingently

---

2 Chronicles 36:14-23
Ephesians 2:4-10
John 3:14-21

I still remember the excitement felt when, in my senior year in college, I read H. Richard Niebuhr's *Meaning of Revelation*. Believing as I did that no intellectually compelling account of Christianity could be given because I could not see how our destiny could be based on a historically contingent fact, I devoured Niebuhr's book. Here not only was an honest mind but one that met, in a constructive and existentially compelling manner, what I thought to be the most decisive challenge to the Christian faith. Even though I later came to doubt the distinction between inner and outer history, to be suspicious of Niebuhr's attempt to combine Troeltsch and Barth, and to distrust Niebuhr's confessionalism, I am forever grateful that at one point in my life I was ready to read that book in a manner that I am sure changed my life.

This was not the first time I had read *Meaning of Revelation*. I read it when I was a senior in high school well before I had ever heard the names of Lessing, Troeltsch, or Barth. Reading it that first time did little for me, as I had no idea why there was a problem about history. Yet reading the book four years later made me so excited I actually trembled. I remember I read it straight through in one sitting.

The experience I describe is not unique. We all have moments and times in our lives when we seem disposed to hear, see, and understand what at another time we would not have noticed. Sometimes it is a novel—perhaps not even a very good novel—that says just the words we need to hear; it may be a painting that helps us to see what we had been looking at but failed to see; or, as is often the case, it is another person who comes into our lives at the right moment, helping us to see, as well as own, the direction of our lives or even to change directions.

What is so unusual about these experiences is how contingent factors converge in a manner that gives them the feeling of necessity. It was a matter of chance that I ever got so bent out of shape that the problem of history, and in particular the question of the "historical Jesus," ever became a problem for me. If Pleasant Mound Methodist Church in

> *Contingent factors converge in a manner that gives them the feeling of necessity.*

Pleasant Grove, Texas, had not had so many young people called to the ministry during the time I was growing up, the idea that I ought to take all this religious stuff seriously would have never occurred to me. Moreover, if I had just been saved some Sunday night, I probably would not have thought it necessary to dedicate my life to the ministry as a substitute—a self-chosen commitment that for the good of God's Church I was soon led to disavow and subsequent history has confirmed my decision. If I had not had a girlfriend back in high school, I probably would have gone to Hendrix College in Conway, Arkansas, rather than South-western University, where I encountered a teacher who knew, in Buber's characterization of the ultimate act of teaching, "when to raise his finger at the right time." If my girlfriend back in Dallas had not jilted me soon after I left, I probably would not have sublimated my lust into a passion for philosophy. If Niebuhr had not been so possessed by the problem of relativism, *Meaning of Revelation* would not have been written. If, when he wrote *Meaning of Revelation,* he had been as critical of Barth's alleged Christomonism, as he was to be later, the book would have lacked the theological tension that makes it so exciting. All that conspired and came together in Georgetown, Texas, sometime in 1962, which is why you are pondering these words on a page.

Our lives are made up of contingencies. We are the result of accidents. We tell ourselves that what we are is what we have made ourselves—after all, I did decide to read *Meaning of Revelation.* Yet we know and fear that we are more affected by what happens to us than by what we do. Even more, we fear the many lost opportunities we have missed because we were not ready to hear this truthful word or because that word was put in a way we were not ready to hear. In short, we fear that for most of our lives we dwell in darkness and have no means even to know that we so dwell.

This is the reason, moreover, that we Christians of modernity have such a fascination with John 3:16—"For God so loved the world that he gave his only Son, so that everyone who believes in him may not perish but may have eternal life." Here it seems we have the gospel—the Good News—so succinctly stated that it should be available to anyone no matter what his or her life circumstance might be. The gospel, we believe, is a universal truth ready to be appropriated by anyone at any place and at any time. Thus John 3:16 now appears nearly every time an extra point is kicked in professional football.

The alleged universal truth embodied by John 3:16, of course, is that God is love. Moreover, we know that this truth involves a bit of unpleasant news: Most of us are not as good or as loving as we think we ought to be, and again, this is a truth anyone is capable of acknowledging. But the good news is that God does not hold our insufficiencies against us. All we have to do is believe in Jesus, a belief that can take many different forms, and we will have eternal life—or, given our doubts about eternity, at least a meaningful life, which is about as close as we can come to the idea of salvation. After all, if we are going to go to the trouble of believing in God—something had to start all this—then we might as well believe that God is also a God of love.

After the gospel is reduced to the formula of John 3:16 one wonders why we need Jesus at all and in particular, why anyone would have ever bothered to have put him to death. Note that this is not the standard catechism question of why Jesus had to die, with its equally standard response—namely as an expiation for our sins. Rather the question is why would anyone ever have gotten upset with Jesus if all he had to tell us is that God loves us and does not want us to perish. I would think anyone with that urgent message would end up with quite a following. Rather Jesus ended on a cross, abandoned by all his followers except for his mother, his mother's sister, Mary the wife of Clopas, Mary Magdalene, and some mysterious figure called "the blessed disciple." How could someone with the message of "pure and unbounded love" end up in such a sorry state? Some terrible mistake must have been made.

A mistake has been made, of course, but the mistake is our attempt to make John 3:16 into a truth of which Jesus' life and death are only illustrations. For God's love is not some generalized attitude that names someone always ready to accept, to forgive, but rather the concrete fleshy love that comes in the person of Jesus of Nazareth. It is in this person that God's love is revealed. It is in this person that God is glorified—glorified through the cross. For as we are told in John 3:14, just as Moses lifted up the serpent in the wilderness, so must the Son of man be lifted up— lifted up in the form of a cross, so that God's arms might be spread wide in order that the world might be embraced into the kingdom.

Yet the hard and harsh truth is that a cross-formed love brings judgment. That light which is meant to illumine, which came not to condemn, creates darkness. How can this be? How can a gospel of "pure unbounded love" create darkness? Moreover, it is a black, thorough, and complete darkness because the Son has now come. Just as a light makes the gray recesses of a room all the darker, so the sending of the Son makes the darkness of the world and our lives darker and more complete. An odd result, it would seem, for a God that is supposed to be about the saving of us.

This should make us think twice about what we mean by salvation. The salvation we want to ensure by abstracting John 3:16 from the life, death, and resurrection of Jesus is a salvation on our terms—it is a gnostic salvation based on the allegedly universal knowledge that God is love. For we think that we know what love is— that we know what it means for God to love the world—and we are very glad indeed to think that what we mean by love is confirmed by God's sending Jesus into the world.

> *The salvation we want to ensure by the abstracting of John 3:16 from the life, death, and resurrection of Jesus is a salvation on our terms—it is a gnostic salvation based on the allegedly universal knowledge that God is love.*

We thus pretend that we are always ready to respond to God, that we are always ready to acknowledge and live in the light cast by the sending of the Son. Salvation is not like the rest of our lives—namely, it is not contingent on our being able to see or hear God's word in the contingent form of Jesus of Nazareth. We may not be ready to understand Niebuhr's *Meaning of Revelation;* we may not be ready to acknowledge that we hate our mother; we may not be prepared to face the fact that we are going to spend all of our lives in ministry; but we think we are always ready to believe that God so loved the world.

We thus use John 3:16 to defeat the terrible knowledge that God's salvation is as contingent as our lives. Put differently, we want to believe that when it comes to salvation, we are always in a position ready to respond to God's grace. Thus almost all contemporary theology has been extraordinarily gracious about God's grace, wanting to ensure that all people, even ourselves, have it irrespective of the darkness in which we dwell. In doing so, ironically, such theology attributes to us a status that only God has. Only God lives noncontingently, and that is why only God can save using the contingent—that is, only God can save through the calling of Israel and the life, death, and resurrection of Jesus Christ.

A darkness is created by the sending of the Son—a darkness, moreover, that we love since we believe that darkness to be the light. Even more we are told we hate the light, not wanting our evil deeds exposed—deeds that are formed by our presumption that we are in control of our existence, even to the point of being in control of our salvation. We thus believe ourselves eternally ready to respond to the light, to the knowledge that God is love, finding it impossible to believe we might really be dwelling in a darkness that we cannot even see because we call it light. We thus are not ready to face the truth that this love is almost violent as it comes wrenching us from the world we have come to love.

The Good News, however, is that because God has sent the Son we do not have to continue to dwell in the darkness. The Good News is that the salvation wrought in Christ allows us to acknowledge that we have loved the darkness without that knowledge of our bent loves destroying us. Because God sent his only Son, we can trust God not to destroy us, even though we have killed the very One who would save us. Forgiven, we are able to look back on our sins, confessing them, no longer fearing that without our sins we will not be.

In that sense, confessing our sin is not unlike recognizing that our life is contingently constituted. We have an almost irresistible desire to turn the contingencies of our lives into necessity. We therefore say that our missed opportunities really worked out for the best. It is a good thing that I did not marry Joe or Mary, for otherwise I would not have had the opportunity to be this or that. In like manner, we fear letting go of our sin exactly because we fear we will have no life if we open our lives to the life of this man Jesus. But by opening our lives we discover that we have no reason to fear the contingent character of our lives, for it has now been made part of God's very life.

This new life is a gift that creates its own response, called, as we learn in Ephesians, faith. Faith names the new reality, the new history, that has been made possible in Christ. It is, moreover, a history that is cosmic in scope because it ensures that all ages are now constituted by the sending of the Son. The love that sends the Son is the same love that moves the sun and the stars.

The cosmic dimensions of God's love ensure that the love that is found in this Jesus can never be exhausted. We will find the book that was so significant at one time to be limited, if not just wrong; we will find our enthusiasm for an artist to be inappropriate in light of his or her later work or our increasing sense of the tragic; we will even find that some people, who in the past were decisive for the direction of our lives, cannot be part of our future. The Good News, however, is that the Son of man that God has lifted up is inexhaustible. Contingent though our lives are, God, through the sending of the Son, fits each of us into a life, into a love, that has no limits, exactly because it is a life contingent as our own. What could be better news than this—that as creatures we have been given the means to live in the light radiating from the cross of Christ?

As those who desire to live in that light, God has entrusted us with this gospel so that the world might know the kind of love that moves the sun and the stars. "For we are what he has made us, created in Christ Jesus for good works, which God prepared beforehand to be our way of life" (Ephesians 2:10). We are the significant book, the magnificent painting, the crucial person necessary for the world to see, for the world to smell, for the world to touch the one who has wrought our salvation. For God's salvation is a contingent, fleshy business. It is as real as the bread and wine that we must eat to live, as real as the one next to us whose very body pulls us into communion so that we might together stand in the truth. Therefore let us not hesitate to share this heavenly feast constituted by earthly fare, assured when we do so that we participate with Christ and all the saints in God's eternal life.

9

The August Partiality of God's Love

Ruth 2:1-13
Matthew 22:34-46

O nce long ago, on the death of his wife, a man
decided to join a particularly austere monastic
order. After placing his two young sons under the
care of the monks, he spent two years as a novice. Before
allowing him to take final vows, the monks brought him to
the drawbridge over the moat surrounding the monastery
and threw his sons into the water. If he had tried to save
them from drowning he would have been judged lacking
in the kind of love necessary to be a monk—that is, his
particular love for his sons would have revealed he was still
in the grip of worldly attachments.

This story offends us. We think the monks' behavior
cruel and inhuman. Yet, in fact, we believe the love
required by the Great Commandment, particularly regard-
ing social questions, is characterized by a similar impartiality. Do we not believe that the love of neighbor requires us
to treat starving children in Africa as if they were our own
children? Or, put another way, do we not believe, though
we do not act accordingly, that we should treat our own
children as if they were anyone's children? Each of us is
equally valuable in God's sight. We do not love as God

loves—that is, treating each person impartially—but we think we ought to so love.

That is why we think the love commandment so demanding—after all, it is no great thing to ask us to love ourselves because that comes with the territory. It is loving ourselves and the neighbor impartially that is

> *Because impartiality is such a demanding ethic, we think it equivalent to agape.*

the hard part. We are convinced that Kant and the utilitarians are right, though each in quite different ways, when they assert that the very heart of morality is that we should treat our interests, even our own loves, as no more valuable than anyone else's interests and loves. Because impartiality is such a demanding ethic, we think it equivalent to agape. To love all equally will certainly require the sacrifice of our own interests and perhaps even the interests of those we love in particular. We are to love our neighbor as ourselves, as God loves—that is, sacrificially. We are not too far removed from the monks.

This interpretation of the love required by the commandment is particularly powerful for those called to the ministry. They are to give their lives in service to others. Yet we know that we are not up to so living as an ongoing project. This results in a classic double bind where the very job description that pastors accept cannot help making them feel like failures. The language of sacrifice also catches women in a particular bind because too often it is but an ideology for further domination. So we think that such love is possible only when we have achieved equality of power in all human relations. This is a difficult agenda because the achievement of such equality seems so unlikely.

No one struggled more with the difficulty of loving all

with the impartiality of God's love than Reinhold Niebuhr. For Niebuhr saw clearly that we cannot love all disinterestedly. In any situation where we must love more than one, we necessarily will have to care for one more than another. Never one to back away from harsh implications, Niebuhr saw that this means, at times, we may even have to kill in order to protect some that we love from others that we should but cannot love in the same way. We must sacrifice our desire to love all impartially, being satisfied that the best we can achieve in this life is justice. That is why Niebuhr never tires of reminding us that the agape of the cross always judges our partial achievements of justice.

I think the power of Niebuhr's influential account helps explain, ironically, the development of a new kind of hypocrisy. Convinced that love must find expression primarily as justice in social relations—that is, love means we must serve as many as possible by changing the structures of injustice—many of us now consider ourselves morally exemplary because we adhere to enlightened sets of social principles. We vote according to these principles, but they seldom require anything of us personally. Too many of us feel that we have an adequate social identity because we hold "right" views about matters such as ecology, feminism, racism, socialism, and war. Such views seldom ask us to change our lives, yet we feel morally superior to those who actually spend their lives caring, for example, for one mentally handicapped child because the latter are ideologically unsound, failing to understand that justice should make us work for the elimination of widespread inequities in society.

> *Many of us now consider ourselves morally exemplary because we adhere to enlightened sets of social principles.*

I have dwelt on this understanding of the impartial love, so often associated with the Great Commandment, because I think it is rooted so deeply in our souls. But I am equally certain it is a false and even demonic understanding of the love that we are to have for God and one another. To so interpret Jesus' command to love is to separate the command from the commander. It is often pointed out that the Great Commandment is not unique to Jesus. Maybe he put them together for the first time, but whether he did or did not is of little importance. More important, we only learn to love God rightly by imitating the love God has shown us through this Jesus of Nazareth.

To turn the Great Commandment into a general admonition of impartiality or self-sacrifice is a moralistic attempt to make the gospel a universal truth that can be known separate from becoming a disciple of Jesus. It is an attempt, in spite of the genuine austerity of impartial love, to make love and God subject to our will and open to our manipulation. For God as the impartial lover is

> *To turn the Great Commandment into a general admonition of impartiality or self-sacrifice is a moralistic attempt to make the gospel a universal truth that can be known separate from becoming a disciple of Jesus.*

no more than the ultimate bureaucrat treating all persons and cases fairly. But we know, for all their fairness, bureaucrats cannot help being unjust because they are unable to see that the differences between us make it impossible to treat us all equally. Moreover, we know that the bureaucracies justified in the name of impartiality cloak unjustified power arrangements that make some more equal than others. So we seek ways to manipulate a god of impartiality, believing by doing so we are making God's bureaucracy more humane.

Yet as much as we might desire to be loved impartially, the God we find in the cross and resurrection does not love us so. Rather the God of Israel and Jesus loves with a passionate particularity, with an august partiality. God loves Israel, God loves Jesus, and God loves the Church with a love of fierce intensity and particularity. God's love is no universal possibility always available in principle, but the love that comes through a history so that our individual importance is acknowledged. God loves us in such a way that our lives—who we are and what we do—matter for God's life. This is not a love subject to our manipulation. God loves us with unrelenting passion that promises to transform the beloved, making us capable of accepting such love. Like all great loves, such love frightens us as we fear we will lose ourselves within it, rather than discovering our true destiny.

On these matters we are at the heart of the greatest mystery of our faith—the Trinity. For what we experience in the august partiality of God's love is how the Father, in loving the Son and Spirit, does not diminish God's capacity to love, but rather makes possible an unfathomable love. As a result, God is able to love each of us in our particularity without diminishing our particularity or lessening God's ability to love another. In God's love of us we do not cease being Jew or Greek, male or female, or the ultimate ontological categories—Texan and everyone else—but rather God's love of us only intensifies our particularity as we are made precious in God's life. God would have each of us citizens of God's kingdom, such that our differences might contribute to the growth of that kingdom.

Why, then, do we persist in resisting loving as God loves—loving ourselves well, as well as loving others in all their particularity? I suspect our resistance comes from two main sources. First, by refusing to love ourselves we create a false righteousness, convincing ourselves that we are not worthy of such love. As a result, we lack the ability to be a friend so long as we refuse to live our lives well enough to be our own best friend. Secondly, and more significantly, our failure to so love reflects our distrust of God. We fear that if we love partially then no one, not even God, will love those whom we cannot love. After all, we only have so much energy. We cannot, like God, love each person differently. Better then to love all impartially. Impartiality is thus the concession we and the world make for our inability to love particularly and partially and intensely. The problem only occurs when we confuse the concession with the love we are to have for God, ourselves, and our neighbor.

But we are not the world. We are God's people. We believe we can risk loving as passionately as God loves. For we know that the love that God makes possible is no scarce resource that must be hoarded so that it can be distributed in dribs and drabs—a little here and a little there. Love is not a rare commodity, but rather the more we love with the intense particularity of God's love, the more we discover that we have the capacity to love. God does not ask us to be God, but rather passionately to love one another with the august partiality we find in Jesus, trusting that God will use our partial loves to expand his kingdom.

Such love is not unlike Wendell Berry's contrast of ballroom dancing with square dancing in his *Home Economics.* Both are obviously sexual, but the former, Berry suggests, is the dance of the capitalist—we dance only with our own. In the square dance, however, we start with our own and then from the intensity of that pairing we are sent out to couple, to be sure not in the same way as with our primary partner, but nonetheless sent out to be with others. We are then rejoined, enriching the intensity of our original pairing by the movements we have learned as we have passed through one another's lives. Similarly, we are to learn to love one another as Christians, believing that in the process the wonderful dance of God's kingdom becomes even more grand and beautiful.[1]

It is the dance we see in the lives of Naomi and Ruth. Ruth, a Moabite, risked much by remaining faithful to the particularity of the history of her marriage to the son of Elimelech. Naomi, with equal partiality, schemed well to place Ruth in the path of Boaz, to sleep at his feet, so that even Boaz found a way to claim Ruth as wife. Through these extraordinarily determined women God engrafted those who were not Israel into the lineage that gave birth to our Savior. In Ruth we see prefigured the engrafting of us—Gentiles—into the fierce partiality of God's love so that the world might know that the God who moves the sun and the stars is also the God who loves Israel, Jesus, and you and me.

That is the love, of course, that makes possible the meal that we share. For in the Eucharist we do not love one another impartially, but rather we come celebrating the partiality of God's love for us that makes possible a community that can risk, indeed even demand, that we learn to love one another in the manner that God has loved us. In the feast we share not love in general, but rather the particularity of our loves, trusting that through such loves God expands our souls, making us capable of welcoming the stranger who often comes in the form of a male, female, Greek, Gentile, or our own children. Is it any wonder, therefore, that the world can only marvel at our love feast, no longer capable of asking questions, overcome with how we have come to love one another through the august partiality of God's love?

10

On the Production and Reproduction of the Saints

Daniel 7:1-3, 15-18
Ephesians 1:11-23
Luke 6:20-36

Across the empty blackness of the cosmos strides Luke Skywalker engaged in a life-and-death struggle with the evil empire. Suddenly space—that terrifying emptiness that is so dark, that so dwarfs us—becomes the backdrop for the ongoing story of the conflict between good and evil. We thrill at the adventure of *Star Wars* as our imaginations are empowered to reclaim the cosmos as part of our life. The planets, stars, the wind, and creatures who are neither animal nor human become animate, serving as they must the good, for otherwise they come under the power of evil.

Our remembering the saints only makes sense against a similar cosmic background. For we Christians believe that the universe—the cosmos—is caught in a struggle even more dramatic than that depicted in *Star Wars*. It is the kind of struggle described in the book of Daniel as created by the beasts who would rule our lives arising from the power of the wind and water. These beasts are terrifying, for like the emperor of the evil empire in *Star Wars*, they know that they are in a life-and-death struggle, and they play for keeps. It is a conflict more serious than life and death. The battle is over who will rule and what the character of that rule will be. We remember the saints because they are our best weapons in this ongoing battle.

Books like Daniel, which we label apocalyptic literature, have not exactly been central for the way we have learned to think as modern Christians. Perhaps that is why we are so starved for stories like *Star Wars*. There is no genre in Scripture that seems more ready for a little demythologizing than apocalyptic literature. Apocalyptic thought, after all, has always been the breeding ground of Christian fanaticism and speculation about who is or is not this or that beast. While I have no wish to underwrite every form of speculation in Christian history inspired by apocalyptic world views, I do want to maintain that our faith—in particular, our holding up the lives of the saints—cannot make sense without the apocalyptic drama of the cosmos in conflict.

When we lose the cosmic character of our faith, the saints are reduced to being saintly—that is, people who are eternally nice. These are people who are always ready to forgive, to sacrifice their own interests for others, who are gentle and kind—they usually like animals. Such people do not look very much like those capable of ruling the four great beast-kings of Daniel. Saints capable of receiving the Kingdom of the Most High, I suspect, are going to be just about as terrifying as beast-kings. Indeed they may even be less than good and in fact, as we know from history, are often capable of doing rather terrible things.

The apocalyptic nature of our faith, its cosmic presumption, reminds us that sainthood is about power. If you are in a struggle—a conflict that engages the forces of the universe—then you need some powerful people at your side. You need some patrons. That, of course—as Peter Brown reminds us in his book *Cult of the Saints*—is exactly how

Christians used to think of saints. They were women and men of power, capable of protecting this small and relatively uninteresting group of people called Christians. Christians, after all, need protection because the world is ruled by beast-kings who want to destroy all those who are witnesses to Jesus' triumph over the powers that would falsely rule the cosmos.

Christians, after all, need protection because the world is ruled by beast-kings who want to destroy all those who are witnesses to Jesus' triumph over the powers that would falsely rule the cosmos.

We are told in Ephesians that before the foundations of the world, God chose us in Jesus so that we might be holy. The whole cosmos is ordered to the glory of this man's resurrection, for there, in the fullness of time, all things in heaven and all things on earth are united. It is this power that the saints inherit:

> Christ when [God] raised him from the dead and seated him at his right hand in the heavenly places, far above all rule and authority and power and dominion, and above every name that is named, not only in this age but also in the age to come. And he has put all things under his feet and has made him head over all things for the church, which is his body, the fullness of him who fills all in all. (Ephesians 1:20-23)

Like it or not, this is apocalyptic language because our God is a cosmic God. We are not asked to choose between nature and history—our God fuses what we call nature and what we call history into the one great drama of the redemption of the cosmos now accomplished in Jesus' bodily resurrection. That is the great Good News of the gospel that we celebrate by remembering the saints. For by being people capable of remembering the saints we claim to be Church—that is, those who have been made part of God's cosmic adventure called kingdom. I assume that you, like me, are at once thrilled and frightened to be so identified. We come to Jesus seeking meaning for our lives, and we discover this Jesus business is about power and conflict on a scale so vast we hardly seem to matter. Yet matter we do because we must be capable of remembering, and perhaps even being, saints.

Of course you may well object to all this cosmic-power language. We Christians, after all, are not about power but about being weak. Attend to the Lukan Beatitudes. The blessed are the poor, the hungry, those who weep, those who are hated and cast out on account of their loyalty to the Son of Man. And look at who are in trouble—the rich, the full, the happy. Moreover we Christians are to love and forgive our enemies, not hate them. This does not sound like conflict and power language.

Yet I am afraid that you have named the problem—namely that we no longer hear the Beatitudes as the constitution of a new people of a new age, as the politics that manifests God's power. The Beatitudes do not say, "Try to be poor, try to be hungry, try to weep." Rather they say blessed are they who are such because they are well positioned for the conflict. We are not told that if we just forgive or love our enemies, they will cease being our enemies. Forgiving enemies is not a subtle way of winning through making our enemies guilty, but rather is only possible because we believe that all

> *Forgiving enemies is not a subtle way of winning through making our enemies guilty.*

things have been put under the dominion of the one who defeated the powers through a cross—the same powers who would rule this world by hate, envy, and violence and because of their weakness must appear rich, full, and without care.

Remembering saints today—saints who seem to be powerless by the world's standards—is part of the ongoing cosmic conflict. Saints ready to forgive enemies often meet untimely ends. God does not promise us that if we forgive our enemies they will repent—they merely may kill us, and even worse, those we love. Yet, though they may kill us, they cannot determine the meaning of our deaths, and so the beast-kings lose. For our saints do not die as victims, but as martyrs. God gives the Church the power through our remembering of the saints to wrench their lives from the tyranny of the oppressor's history so they triumph over the forces of death. In God's memory the saints triumph.

That is why we cannot try to be saints. God produces the saints, and they are reproduced through us. God makes us possible through production of the saints. They are our material-factor, and we thus are surprised to discover that we, the rememberers, have been made into Church. Through remembering the saints we have become part of the cosmic conflict, but we can rejoice because we know the hope to which we have been called through the glorious inheritance of the saints.

Saints, therefore, are not Luke Skywalkers—that is, they are not heroes or heroines. Rather they are people like us who have been made more than we are by being engrafted into God's kingdom that is ruled by the power of forgiveness and love. Even though we rightly remember particular Christians' lives for sustaining our part in God's adventure, we are mindful that it is God that makes their and our lives possible. So we celebrate the saints—and we should each name some for ourselves—but that celebration is about the victory of God alone who triumphed over the beast-kings.

Therefore, all of us who hunger can come now and feed at the meal of memory. The meal is our imagination as we become characters in God's drama of salvation. So we leave our weeping behind and join in the cosmic hilarity that God has made possible for us, the saints. Here, we come into possession of the kingdom hard won, but surely won by our Savior risen from the dead. Here, those who would rule through terror and violence come to ruin. So we come to a powerful feast where we are joined in communion with all God's saints who by God's grace have learned to rejoice in the beauty of a cosmos ordered to God's rule. This is the feast of victory of our God who has made us saints.

11

On Being De-Possessed:

Or This Is a Hell of a Way to Get Someplace

Genesis 3:8-19
Hebrews 4:1-3, 9-13
Mark 10:17-30

very now and then I think I need to "pare down"—
to get rid of some of my stuff so I might be able to
travel a little lighter. When I am in this mood I am
even able to throw a few things away. It is usually stuff I
thought I needed at one time but am now convinced I do
not need, since I literally have not even picked the stuff up
for years. However, it's hard to throw or give away even
some of that kind of stuff because you never know when
you are going to need that old waffle iron. After all, much
of this stuff is like an old friend. I find in my case that this
is particularly true of books. I may never read Trollope's
Belton Estate again, but knowing it is on my shelf comforts
me. I could no more give it away than I can afford to lose a
friend.

I am actually able to get rid of a lot of stuff when I have
to move. Faced with the choice of having to pack it and
move it or to let Goodwill haul it off, Goodwill often wins.
However, moving is not good news when it comes to par-

ing down. I move to a new place, and it has a bigger yard, so I have to buy a power mower, and if I have to have a power mower, then I have to have a gas can—and before long I discover I have more stuff.

This tendency for us to acquire more and more things is particularly true in our society, and I expect is particularly troubling for those who have money. For us, if you've got it, it is immoral not to spend it. If you do not spend it, you throw people out of work. You can talk all you want about learning to do with less or our need to create a smaller world, but if we do not learn to want and need more things, the result is that some people will be out of a job. Getting rid of possessions is no easy matter.

> *I must admit that I would rather have an attitude problem about a Porsche than my Toyota station wagon.*

We need, as a result, to be careful not to moralize Mark 10—that is, to turn it into text that can be applied to our lives in a rather direct fashion. For example, some are tempted to read this text as an incipient pre-Marxist attack on the rich. That seems all right as long as I do not have to think of myself as rich, but then some suggest that the problem is deeper because the issue is possessions themselves. So the text is not about how much you own before you are rich—does owning a house count?— but rather the issue is any possession, whether we are rich or middle class, that has power to possess us. The issue is not about possessions in and of themselves, but rather about our attitude toward our possessions. If that is the case, I must admit that I would rather have an attitude problem about a Porsche than my Toyota station wagon.

This manner of construing the text has the virtue of reminding us that dispossessing is no easy matter. Few of us know how to dispossess. It is a little like learning how to be unselfish or humble. The more I try to be self-effacing, the more self-involved I become. Possessed by what Iris Murdoch has called the "fat relentless ego," we discover that our very attempts to deny or repress those egos only result in more subtle and fatal forms of self-absorption.

So learning to live without possessions is not some general truth about how to get through life with less trouble or put another way, learning to "travel light." I suspect generally we would all be better off if we learned to travel lighter, but I do not think that is what Mark 10 is about. Rather this text reminds us that we are on a journey. Not just any journey, but a journey that begins with a very particular beginning and ends with an equally definite end— "And as he was setting out on a journey, a man ran up and knelt before him, and asked him, 'Good Teacher, what must I do to inherit eternal life?'" After the exchange with this man and further reflection with the disciples about the status of the rich, we are told:

> They were on the road, going up to Jerusalem, and Jesus was walking ahead of them; they were amazed, and those who followed were afraid. He took the twelve aside again and began to tell them what was to happen to him, saying, "See, we are going up to Jerusalem, and the Son of Man will be handed over to the chief priests and the scribes, and they will condemn him to death; then they will hand him over to the Gentiles; they will mock him, and spit upon him, and flog him, and kill him; and after three days he will rise again."

Put bluntly—that is a hell of a way to get someplace. If I were one of the disciples, I would be thinking, "I thought we were supposed to get somewhere by following this guy, only it does not sound like anywhere I wanted to go." This is not the kind of movement I thought we were about.

We cannot help being sympathetic with the disciples. On hearing how hard it is for the rich to be saved, we too want to say, "Then who can be saved?" or we begin to worry if we are poor enough. Like the disciples, we get very defensive, noting, "Look here Jesus—we've left everything to follow you. I was a pretty good fisherman, had a nice family, even was considering adding a room on to the house. But I left it all for you." Much to our surprise, moreover, Jesus does not propose that you have not done enough yet. Rather he says, "That is good"—just as it is good that the young man has kept the commandments. Even more, he suggests that all that we have given we will get back a hundredfold. Like Job we are going to go through some tough times, but, by God, we are going to be rewarded—in this age and the age to come.

We have to admit that we are a little embarrassed that Jesus responds to the disciples' protestations in this manner. We have learned to despise those who do the right thing in order to get a future reward.

> *Why make Christianity into a grand utilitarian scheme that corrupts the gospel and our lives?*

Why make Christianity into a grand utilitarian scheme that corrupts the gospel and our lives? We are called to be Christians not in order to get eternal life, but because it is a good in and of itself. Moreover, our concern in this regard seems right because we rightly think that those who live righteously for wrong reasons cannot be trusted. We are not virtuous for some reward beyond virtue. If virtue is not its own reward—if the life of goodness is not intrinsic to itself—then we live wrongly.

That is true, I think, but it also reflects a decisive misunderstanding of the journey that Jesus invites us to begin. It is the same kind of misunderstanding that is behind the idea that Jesus is asking us to give up our possessions if we are to follow him to Jerusalem. Both are forms of human pretensions that fail to trust in the power of God to make possible what would have otherwise been impossible.

To understand this we must direct our attention to Jesus' death—to his crucifixion. Jesus tells us that the "Son of Man" will be delivered up, mocked, scourged, and killed—only to be raised. "Only to be raised" sounds like "You are going to get everything back a hundredfold." It sounds as if Jesus knew he was going to have some hard times, but everything was going to come out all right. I suggest to you that if in fact that is what Jesus meant, then this Jesus is a false messiah and we should not follow him one minute more. Such a Jesus could only be the docetic idol—an idol, to be sure, many want in order to ensure that their lives have meaning hopefully in this world or at least the next. But that is a docetic Jesus who could not die on the cross.

For Jesus too, like us, had to be dispossessed. Jesus, like us, had to have his profoundest desires denied. Jesus had to pioneer the journey that could only result in the ultimate loss of possession—which was not his life since Jesus, like us, knew he must die, but rather the possibility that God's kingdom had not come. This man came proclaiming the time of God's kingdom. This man came asking others to act irresponsibly because of that proclamation, to leave everything—job, house, wife, children—because now God's kingdom is aborning. This kingdom, moreover, would defeat the powers that possess this world through our possessions.

A heady ambition indeed. Yet Jesus had to go to the cross—abandoned by the crowd; abandoned by the leader of his people, Israel; abandoned by his disciples—kept company only by his mother and a few women. But even more terrible, he was abandoned to death and death's kingdom by God—abandoned by the very One who made his life and proclamation of the kingdom possible.

But what was not possible was done—God in a mighty new creation raised Jesus from the dead. This is not the resuscitation of a corpse but rather the vindication of this life as the very presence and power of God's kingdom here and now. Dispossessed, Jesus is possessed by the same power that made possible his birth and life, so that now through the resurrection we may properly worship him. Only God is good, only God deserves worship, and now we rightly call Jesus the Son of God.

Because Jesus has made this journey we cannot, and need not, die his death. Praise God for that because it is upon his death our salvation depends. Yet, because we can trust that death, we can also trust our lives to his kingdom by setting out on the journey that is that kingdom. By so doing we can trust that, though unable to dispossess ourselves, with God all things are possible. For we will discover that once we are on the way, the adventure of the kingdom is so compelling that we fail to notice the possessions that we have given up. We discover that ironically through being dispossessed, we are given life anew, which makes possible an enjoyment we did not know was possible. For in Jesus' death and resurrection the New Age has come—eternal life—which we can enjoy at this time, as we are called once again to share God's life with all the saints—those who have gone before and those who stand among us—in this wonderful movable feast meant to nourish all those on the journey we call the kingdom of God.

12

Sin, Complexity, and Violence

Lenten Sermon
James 4:1-12

Come to Bethel—and transgress;
to Gilgal—and multiply transgression;
bring your sacrifices every morning,
your tithes every three days;
bring a thank-offering of leavened bread,
and proclaim freewill offerings, publish them;
for so you love to do, O people of Israel!
says the Lord GOD. (Amos 4:4)

Amos's satirical words surely do not apply to us—especially at Lent. For Lent—this time of examination, of confession, of repentance, of reconciliation—is not a time we particularly enjoy. Generally we do not relish the idea of proclaiming or publishing our sins, which Lent seems to require. To assess our lives against the background of Christ's passion is not a task to which we look forward any more than we wish to join him on the road to Jerusalem. Therefore, it is hard to see how we can use Lent, as Israel used Bethel and Gilgal, for our own purposes.

But on reflection, I am not so sure that we are not more than a little attracted by Lent. For at the very least, Lent seems to legitimize a self-involvement on our part that is seldom warranted by the gospel. At Lent, I am invited to take myself seriously even if it means taking myself seriously as a sinner. Rigorous self-examination, after all, has the virtue of underwriting the view that at least my sins are of some interest.

Moreover, Lent is attractive because sin itself is attractive. On the whole we are bored people, and we would all be a little sad without our sin. We secretly suspect, after all, that our sin keeps life interesting. Good novelists know that it is almost impossible to write an interesting and compelling novel about someone who is genuinely good.

> *On the whole we are bored people, and we would all be a little sad without our sin.*

Not only is sin interesting, but even better, it is complex, and we revel in its complexity. Therefore, Lent legitimates the search to find how we use humility to conceal pride, how we use our weakness to exert power over another, or how we use our sensuality to hide the fact that we are not courageous enough to desire anything. God, we are subtle sinners—and we thank God for it. We are as complex in our sin as we are in our righteousness, and we would not have it otherwise.

Lent is thus a time when, painful as finding and acknowledging our sin may be, we are at least attracted to the complexity of the task of acknowledging and repenting of our sins. But the very attractiveness of that complexity may in fact be an indication of how deeply we are mired in sin. For we are pridefully impressed with our complexity. Now there is a subtle point. Are you not glad that we noticed it? God, we are clever.

Yet the Scripture does not address us as clever or complex sinners. Rather this strawy—as Luther described it—Epistle of James has all the subtlety of a sledge hammer. It really makes things quite simple and assumes that our sin is quite simple.

"Those conflicts and disputes among you, where do they come from? Do they not come from your cravings that are at war within you? You want something and do not have it; so you commit murder" (James 4:1-2*a*). Now wait just a minute, surely things are more complex than this! Of course, some people kill others sometimes because they have something they want, but that is not the rule. Rather we usually are forced to kill for some cause or ideal or necessity, or we kill to protect others we care about and who need our protection. "You want something and do not have it; so you commit murder." I am afraid James simply will not cut it as an adequate explanation of violence in our world. At the very least you have to acknowledge the insights, for example, that the instincts of the territorial imperative still apply. Moreover there is no direct connection between my desiring and killing. I may have my desires wrong, but there is no evidence that will necessarily result in violence.

But what if James is right? What if the reason that violence is so prevalent among us, that it is so deeply rooted in each of our souls, is precisely because we desire and covet what is not ours, and so we fight and wage war to get it. James is not suggesting that the problem is that we have desires, but he is saying, rather, that the desires we have are for the wrong thing. First we are hesitant to ask; then, asking but not receiving, we are frustrated. And we seek to make someone pay for our frustrations. Yet we are bound to be frustrated because that for which we asked cannot be satisfied, because our wants are formed by passions that only spend and want more. Such must be the case since our passions are formed by our friendships with this world and not with God. Therefore the problem seems to lie in where we find our friends, and in particular our steadfast refusal to accept God's friendship. We thus end by being at war with ourselves and one another.

This is not really the kind of sin that we seek to confess at Lent. This is not the kind of sin we seek to root out of our lives. In many ways it is too mundane and uninteresting. It is not exactly news that we desire the wrong thing. And even more, it scares us to think matters would be this simple and have such terrible consequences—namely, that the violence of the world lies within each of us. What are the causes of war? Our divided desires. A popular response to this answer might be, "Wait just a minute. Do not lay that on me! The causes of wars are complex—historical disputes, national self-interest, economic injustices. Our desires do not create wars!"

But if the causes of wars do lie in our desires, then we do indeed have much to confess, for there is no complexity here. The issue is very clear. We Christians have continued to think that we can be friends with the world and with God, but if we are friends with the world, then indeed we are enemies of God and enemies of one another—we are the source of violence. We prefer that our sins be complex. Indeed, we will willingly publish and multiply them rather than face this humbling. After all, it is very hard for creatures as subtle as ourselves to be humble. But it seems that we must be if we are ever serious about drawing near to God, for "God opposes the proud, but gives grace to the humble" (1 Peter 5:5).

But it is not as if humility is good in and of itself. On the contrary, we are called to be humble in order that we might be friends of a humble God who has chosen to redeem his own, not through coercion but through uncompromising love. Only as we learn to draw near to such a love do we become humble enough to be at peace with ourselves and one another. And without our being so humble we lack the means to be a community of peace, and thus the world lacks any means to know that this is an alternative to violence.

Yet I do not wish to seek the humility to which James calls us, for it requires that I acknowledge a far too horrible truth. The cause of war—the cause of the brutal killing of thousands of women and children, the cause of the devastation of the country that is almost worse than the killing itself—is nothing less than my desire and my covetousness. Surely this

"Of course you do not desire war, but what you desire makes war inevitable."

is wrong. I desire not war. But the uncompromising, simple answer comes back: "Of course you do not desire war, but what you desire makes war inevitable." Do you not desire fame or security or just a little control over someone else? And we wonder why there is fighting among us.

This strawy epistle is beginning to prove more uncompromising than we had anticipated. Surely there is some legalism lurking in all this that will allow us to dismiss it or at least note that what is said here must be balanced by Paul's more theologically profound account of justification. But we cannot get off the hook so easily. For, like Paul, James sees that the issue is the kind of people we Christians are supposed to be—namely, it is not our task to act as if we are the creators of the law or the judges of the law determining which brother or sister is more or less in accordance with the law. It *is* our task to be doers of the law. For only the doers of the law know rightly who the true judge is—the true lord of the world, who is the only basis of peace within ourselves and of one another.

But then indeed we do need this time of Lent. For what

would it mean for us to confess that our desires, the passions that are at war within our members, are in fact the causes of war? And we Christians—who proclaim to the world that we serve a God of peace, a crucified Savior—cannot even be at peace within ourselves. For in fact, we know we do speak evil against one another, and we judge as if we are worthy to judge. In short, we act not as those who need to cleanse our hands or purify our hearts. Rather, we continue to assume pridefully that the very knowledge of the complexity of our sin is but an indication of our righteousness. Like the serpent, most of the time we remain neither very good nor very evil; we are simply subtle. But this subtlety turns out to be the cause of violence and war.

So, brothers and sisters, I tell you that on this day and in this season, in any day and all seasons, we indeed have much for which we must repent. For we have been confronted by a God who calls us to peace, who has shown us what we should clearly desire in singleness of heart, and yet we persist in desiring friendship with the world and its violence. God forgive us.

13

Hating Mothers as the Way to Peace

Ezekiel 33:1-11
Philemon 1-20
Luke 14:25-33

Most of us believe that we are nonviolent. We believe that we would prefer to be peaceable rather than violent in most circumstances of our lives. Violence is something that exists "out there" in criminal behavior or in relations between states. We simply do not believe it is in our souls. Rather violence is in structures of our existence, insofar as they are determined by past and ongoing injustice.

Moreover, there is some basis for this belief. Few of us have ever threatened anyone with physical violence. We may entertain heroic fantasies of responding or employing violence in a good cause, but most of us discover that if we are actually confronted with violence and need to respond in kind, we become physically ill. We simply are not natural killers. We sincerely prefer to live in order rather than the disorder that violence always seems to breed.

Indeed it is very hard to get us to kill. This is true even in war. In World War I, 40 percent of the soldiers in combat never fired their weapons. Thus the military created the platoon system. Friendships are created in platoons that force us finally to use violence in the protection of one another. As J. Glenn Gray notes in his book *The Warriors:* "Numberless soldiers have died more or less willingly, not for country or religious faith or for any other abstract good, but because they realized that by fleeing their post and rescuing themselves, they would expose their companions to greater danger. Such loyalty is the essence of fighting morale."[1] So even in war we discover that we are not violent in ourselves but only because we so care about those we have learned to love by being exposed to a common danger.

In short, we kill to protect others. In that sense, our psychology seems to fit Augustine's defense of the use of violence through war. Augustine argued that it is incompatible for Christians to ever use violence to protect ourselves. Thus, his defense of the just war was never on grounds that it was analogous to self-defense. Rather, Augustine argued that Christians can use violence only to protect the innocent, and by *innocent* he meant only those who did not deserve the attack they were receiving. So the Christian justification of violence derives not from the assumption that we must at times defend ourselves, but rather from the idea that violence is necessary if we are charitably to protect the innocent.

All of which reminds us that our violence lies not in ourselves but in our loves. We think it crucial to protect those we love. Indeed, I suspect most of us go to war to protect our loves. Our families, our neighborhoods, are what we care about when we go to war—nations are but symbols, all too powerfully real symbols to be sure, of those cares.

> *Our violence lies not in ourselves but in our loves.*

Moreover, there seems to be something deeply right about this. It is natural to defend those we love, and we would have little use for people who did not feel that they should defend those they love. Cowardice, in fact, is placing our interest in survival over those we love. It is only on this basis that we can understand why war is such an important moral institution, for without it we would lack the means of sacrifice so crucial for us to know how important our loves are to us.

I suspect that this is the reason that Luke 14 is so jarring. "Whoever comes to me and does not hate father and mother, wife and children, brothers and sisters, yes, and even life itself, cannot be my disciple" (Luke 14:26). On hearing this difficult message, we think that Jesus must surely be speaking figuratively—after all, if Christianity is about anything today we think it must surely be about supporting the family. What Jesus must mean, therefore, is that we must not love our families too much. He is simply recommending that we need to get our priorities right. We should remember that we should not make our families gods, but once we remember that, it is surely right to love our families even to the point of taking the lives of others, if necessary, to defend them.

Yet that is not what Jesus says. He does not merely say that we have our priorities wrong. Rather, he says that now that we are in his presence, all our relations have been transvalued. Through his death and resurrection a great reversal has taken place so that now all of our natural loves must be transformed.

This is the beginning of a New Age—an age of which we do not become part unless we hate mother, hate father, hate wife or husband, and children. This is not just a matter of getting your priorities right. No, it means that now everything has been returned to its original purpose. The New Age is here in the person of Jesus Christ, so we are no longer under the powers of the old age—powers that feed on our fears and our loves, leading us to kill other people's children in the name of protecting our own. Hating mother, father, spouse, and children only makes sense if we now live in a new time when everything is made new, when the wolf now lies down with the lamb, and when we can love our children without threatening the children of others.

Indeed, Jesus argues in a commonsense way that if you were going to build a tower, you would look pretty silly if you began without knowing whether you have the resources to complete it. So if you only get the foundation finished, you will be mocked, as your neighbors will say, "What a silly person to have begun a project without knowing if he had the resources to complete it." As the son of a bricklayer, I can understand just how absurd we would look if we started a project without securing the bricks to finish it.

Or again, Jesus suggests that those who encounter another in war had better make sure that they have an army sufficient to win. To enter war, the most serious of businesses, facing certain defeat would surely be silly. If you confront unfavorable odds, you certainly ought to sue for peace before you begin the battle. Otherwise many people will sacrifice their lives for no good reason.

The point of these examples is not that they are recommendations about how to be a better builder or general, but that if Jesus is the Messiah, it is surely absurd to think we can follow Jesus while clinging to the attachments of the old age. Rather to be his disciple means that all our pasts and all our loves (the loves of our mothers, our fathers, our wives, our husbands, and children) are now made part of a new order. We have become part of a new kingdom that makes it possible for our loves to be the basis of peace rather than the source of violence. For now in this New Age, we love, knowing that our security is in God who has redeemed us through the establishment of his kingdom in Jesus. Now we need not desperately try to ensure the survival of those we love, as we can now love them with the security of the conviction that God's kingdom is surely here. In short, Jesus brought the end-time so that now we have the time to love without that love becoming the source of our violence.

Putting this as dramatically as I can, Jesus' claim about the end-time is equivalent to a nuclear war. Imagine yourself surviving a nuclear war. Imagine yourself being one of the survivors of Hiroshima or Nagasaki. We can hardly imagine what that would feel like, but we know surely everything—even our loves—would be forever changed. Common testimony of those at Hiroshima is that after the bomb they were numb, feeling nothing. Moreover, even as their feelings returned, their lives were forever scarred by that event. Everything they do after is in reference to their being survivors. The bomb has scarred their history, transfiguring past and future. Each must learn to love as a survivor, to be a brother or a sister as a survivor, to be a mother or husband as a survivor. In short, they must learn to cherish one another under the dreadful knowledge of what happened then and perhaps what awaits them in the future.

But as Christians we believe that what happened in Jesus Christ was more dramatic than what happened at Hiroshima or even what would happen if there was a future nuclear exchange. For what happened in Jesus Christ is this: God sent his Son to reclaim his creation and we killed him. It is often said today that there is nothing we could do that is worse than destroying the human species through a nuclear war. That is surely wrong. We have already done the worst thing that we could do. We killed him who would work out our redemption. That is the worst thing that humankind could possibly do.

But the good news is that the God whom we crucified refused to let our no be the final word. God refused to hold this horrible sin against us. Raising Jesus from the grave, God rejects our rejection. Instead, God offers us the opportunity to become part of a new kingdom—of a new time—so that the world might know its true sovereign. It is a time that creates the space for us to learn to love one another so that now our loves will not become the excuse to kill. For now we have learned that the very heart of love is nonviolence because God has come not to coerce us into loving, but to make it possible for us to freely respond to this love, thus making us new creatures.

It is no wonder, therefore, that we believe as Christians that what has happened in Jesus Christ is more significant than a nuclear war. We believe that what has happened in Jesus Christ has changed all our relations. But this bomb that is our redemption does not leave us numb, as the bomb at Hiroshima left the survivors there. Rather, this bomb empowers us to witness to the world the good news that God has rejected our rejection. Instead God uses our sin to offer us a new life, free from the fear that fuels our violence. For now we know that God has removed the violence that once lay in our loves, as we have been taught to love one another now, not in general, but in Christ. Only that love can be the love of peace, for we can love not fearing the loss of love, but confident that now our loves rightly build Christ's kingdom, which is the only alternative to the world's kingdom of war.

This is the gospel. This is what makes it possible for us to be at peace, to be a peaceable people, in a world at war. For we Christians do not believe that we should be peaceable because our peace is a political strategy for freeing the world from war. Rather we Christians know that we must be peaceable, not because our peaceableness will free the world from war, but because our peace is the only way that we can live in a world at war.

That is what we do in Church as we celebrate God's

peace. In the congregation we become brothers and sisters caring for one another in Christ. We care for one another not in family bloodlines, but in Christ. The blood of the cross has forever qualified the blood of the family, making it impossible for us to spill the blood of others in the name of our families. This new eschatological family we call the Church, which now has our fundamental loyalty, makes peace possible even among families.

Much is said today about domestic violence. The causes for this horrible phenomenon are no doubt many and complex. But surely one of the reasons that we seem so incapable of providing an alternative for such violence is that we have no way of providing a paradigm of love that is genuinely peaceable apart from the family. If we are to love one another well in the family—as husbands and wives, as brothers

> *Surely, one of the reasons that we seem so incapable of providing an alterna-tive for such violence is that we have no way of providing a paradigm of love that is genuinely peaceable apart from the family.*

and sisters, as parents and children—we need a sense of a love that is as nonviolent as it is truthful. Such love cannot be real without our families' loves being fundamentally qualified by the love that we learned in the Church.

I am aware that this is an extraordinary and perhaps even frightening thing to say, but then God is a frightening presence. Indeed, from this perspective, I suspect some of us begin to have just a little sympathy with those who put Jesus to death. How dare Jesus tell me to hate my father, my mother, my spouse and especially my children! Yet that is exactly what he said we must do if we are to be part of God's kingdom of peace and love. For any love that does not love the other in relation to the God who has loved us is now accursed. Any love that does not love in the manner that God loves us in Jesus of Nazareth will only be the cause of our violence—providing, as it does, the needed rationale to unleash the vengeance of the wrongs others do to those we love.

This is indeed a difficult message. As we learn from the passage in Ezekiel, God's watchman can be tempted not to sound the warning. Moreover, if we fail to warn, then the very iniquity of those we are called to warn is ours. These are frightening words indeed for those of us who would bear the name Christian. For we believe Christ has made us God's Church, the watchman for the world. Our task is to sound the horn so that the world might be warned that its ways lead only to its own destruction.

Yet the prevalence of violence in the world, the *mad* situation in which we find ourselves in regard to nuclear weapons, is but a sign of the Church's failure to be God's watchman, to be God's horn blower. The Church's task is not to warn the world that it stands on the brink of destroying itself through nuclear war. The world knows that. You can read about that in the *New York Times*. Rather the Church's task is to tell the world that the reason it is so violent is because of its unbelief and that its loves are thereby perverted. For the world does not believe that Jesus has, in fact, risen, making present a New Age and thus transforming our lives. The world does not believe in a God that refuses to let our rejection of Jesus determine our relations to God and to one another. We must say to the world, as watch-

> *Rather the Church's task is to tell the world that the reason it is so violent is because of its unbelief and that its loves are thereby perverted.*

men, that we see the sword and that all the world must turn from unbelief. We must learn to love our lives as gifts and not as possessions. We must learn to love those who are so important to us as gifts from God and not as our possessions. Only then will the world have an alternative to the world's violence.

It is good news indeed, as we hear in Ezekiel, that God takes no pleasure in our death but rather calls us to life as his Church so that the world might know that there is an alternative to our violence. Church statements against nuclear war will do little to make the bomb go away, but that is not the Church's task. Rather her task is to watch and blow the warnings, so that we and the world might know that God has redeemed us in Jesus Christ in such a manner that nothing we can do, even the destruction of the world, can reverse that redemption. Let us praise God for that, even to being led time and time again to God's table of sacrifice, where our loves are transformed so that, rather than being the source of violence, we become the exemplification of God's peace.

14

Lust for Peace

Isaiah 11:6-9
Matthew 5:21-32

I have never liked these verses from Matthew. My dislike for them is not just that they seem so unrealistic, but I do not like their juxtaposition. I can understand Jesus' harsh words about killing and, perhaps, he is even right about anger. But I do not like his taking up in sequence adultery and divorce as if they were morally on a par with killing. I do not mean to deny that adultery may be an important moral issue, but compared with questions of life-taking, what we do or do not do with our genitals is almost trivial.

My disquiet about this text is simply part of my dis-ease with the overemphasis on sexual issues in the Church today. If you attend to recent Christian discourse, it is almost as if the only issue that is important is homosexuality and maybe promiscuity. Given the current condition of the world—that is, given the fact that we may be preparing to blow ourselves up, to invade countries at will—this concentration on sex seems wrong. It is to allow the agenda of the bourgeois to capture our attention in an unjustified manner. Surely all matters of sexual ethics should take a back seat in a war-making world.

So I want to talk about war, and yet I have to talk about sex. It may be, however, that I am wrong to think that I must choose between these topics. For, as I suggested at the beginning, the text in Matthew seems to suggest that issues of killing are on a par with questions of adultery. Might it even be the case that there is some connection between Jesus' admonitions about anger and lust?

Perhaps we need to put the issue even more strongly. For it may be that we find ourselves ill-prepared as Christians to address the issues of war because we have not prepared our-selves well in matters dealing with sex. Can it be that our understand-ing attitude about adul-tery, divorce, and casual sex has made us less able to confront critically the reality of war? It is at least interesting to note that some of the theologians

Some of the theologians and ethicists who argue for more openness in matters sexual are also more willing to justify the necessity of war on utilitarian grounds.

and ethicists who argue for more openness in matters sexual are also more willing to justify the necessity of war on utilitar-ian grounds. Adultery, after all, does sometimes work out for the greatest good of the greatest number; the bombing of Hiroshima resulted in the greater good as fewer lives were lost than if American troops had invaded—at least fewer American lives.

The suggestion that there may be some close connec-tion between our attitude about sex and war was interest-ingly enough suggested by Jonathan Schell in his book *The Fate of the Earth.* It is fascinating, however, that Schell's sug-gestions about the relationships between our views of love, family, sex, and nuclear war have not been discussed as much as other aspects of his deservedly celebrated book. I suspect that the reason is, Schell challenges some of our working assumptions about sexual experience and ethics. Schell's views, when developed, have alarming implications about how we should regard our lives sexually.

Schell builds his case against nuclear war by pointing

out that the biological continuity of the species is made into a human continuity through the institution of marriage. Marriage solemnizes love by providing an outward form for our inward feelings. By swearing their love to one another in public, lovers let it be known that their union is fit for bringing children into the world. Thus, even though marriage is one of the most personal of actions, it is also our most public. For in a world being perpetually overturned by death, marriage lays the foundation for stability. Marriage gives the world a history by transforming biological continuity into familial continuity. Marriage is the way we challenge the dehumanizing threat of death, thus making it possible to view this world as home.

But, according to Schell:

> The peril of extinction surrounds such love with doubt. A trembling world, poised on the edge of self-destruction, offers poor soil for enduring love to grow in. Everything that this love would build up, extinction would tear down. "Eros, builder of citie" (in Auden's phrase, in his poem eulogizing Freud on the occasion of his death) is thwarted. Or, to put it brutally but truthfully, every generation that holds the earth hostage to nuclear destruction lays a gun to the head of its own children. In laying this trap for the species, we show our children no regard, and treat them with indifference and neglect. As for love itself, love lies in the moment, but the moment is dying, as we are, and love also reaches beyond its moment to dwell in a kind of permanence. For
>
> Love's not Time's fool, though rosy lips and cheeks
> Within his bending sickle's compass come;
> Love alters not with his brief hours and weeks,
> But bears it out even to the edge of doom.
>
> But if doom's edge draws close, love's vast scope is narrowed and its resolve may be shaken. The approach of extinction drives love back into its perishable moment, and, in doing so, tends to break up love's longer attachments, which now, on top of all the usual vicissitudes, have the weight of the whole world's jeopardy to bear.[1]

So goes the gospel of Jonathan Schell. And I wonder if his gospel may not be justified in our Gospel reading for this

Adultery, like the bomb, does not look to long-term commitments.

sermon. For at the heart of our Gospel reading is a condemnation of adultery that is not unlike Schell's condemnation of the effect of the nuclear threat on marriage. Adultery, like the bomb, does not look to long-term commitments. It does not seek to endure across generations. Adultery, like the bomb, is action without hope. It seeks no children, for its very form requires that nothing be accomplished beyond the act itself. That does not mean that every act of adultery needs to be construed in a selfish or unloving way. Obviously, adultery is often the result of profound attraction in which each person desires to respond to the needs of the other. From the perspective of the Gospel, that is not the problem. Rather the problem is that adultery by its very nature cannot look forward to any life beyond itself.

But what of the harsh words against divorce? Surely it does not stand on the same footing as adultery. Marriages, after all, go dead. The love of which Schell speaks flickers and goes out. That it does so does not mean the end of marriage but only the end to some marriages. Yet from Schell's and Jesus' perspective, divorce cannot be taken lightly. For if marriage is our public pledge to be related in a manner fit to bring forth and raise children, then surely divorce cannot be easily legitimated. Rather, divorce is a threat to our attempt to form a world that is humane enough in which to raise children. The threat is not, as it is often alleged, that divorce threatens to destabilize our social order. We are stronger than that. Moreover the divorced continue to get married, often to people very much like their former spouses. Habits are hard to break. Rather, the threat is to our moral presuppositions because institutionalization of divorce underwrites our wrong assumptions that we can live without responsibility for our past or for the future.

Therefore, Schell argues that our only hope to challenge the death-affirming assumptions of nuclear extinction is to affirm life, affirm marriage, desire that the unborn exist for their own sake. We must will that new life be continually created, for it is just that life which forces us to attend to the future. "Everything else—our wish to serve the future generations by preparing a decent world for them to live in, and our wish to lead a decent life ourselves in a common world made secure by the safety of the future generations—flows from this commitment. Life comes first. The rest is secondary."[2]

Schell's argument is an attempt to make us conscious of some of the implications of living with the threat of nuclear annihilation. But I wonder if his diagnosis has not put the matter backwards. The attitudes toward marriage and sex, in his view, are the result of our living in fear of a nuclear world. These attitudes were present long before the development of nuclear weapons. The crucial link between marriage and future generations, which are broken by the despair occasioned by the threat of nuclear war, had occurred prior to our ability to blow the world up. It was broken not by the bomb, but by the attempt by many to make sex free from what were perceived to be life-denying restraints inherited from repressive traditions.

Thus our culture believes that sex should not be associated with, nor should it derive its significance from, children. Sex can be whatever you want it to be. It can be good, clean fun. It can be a significant form of relating. It can be an expression of love. It can be important inside and outside of marriage. But there is certainly no intrinsic reason to associate sex with marriage or with the caring for children. Such may have been the case when we lacked effective means of contraception, but now technology has freed us from that biological necessity.

But if Schell is right, these attitudes adopted in the name of affirming life and freedom in matters sexual contain the seeds of our destruction. Once marriage no longer shapes the meaning of sex, we have brought sex under the reign of death. In the name of freedom we have given form to our self-hate and doubt, as our sexual ethic manifests a profound lack of confidence that we have any-

> *Once marriage no longer shapes the meaning of sex, we have brought sex under the reign of death.*

thing worthy to pass on to a new generation. We say we are liberating ourselves from a repressive and tyrannical past, but in fact we are willing our deaths.

Could it possibly be that our attitudes about sex and marriage create the ethos that makes possible a world dominated by the threat of nuclear annihilation? Perhaps Schell has it wrong. Nuclear weapons do not cause us to reject our future, but rather we have rejected our future and thus created the means of our suicide. A people who no longer desire descendants are a people who may well be capable of creating a technology capable of blowing up the world. Indeed the creation of such a technology almost becomes an imperative, for what else can relieve the boredom of lives that have no stake in a future? Sex for fun is interesting for a time, but it is difficult to sustain as a long-term project. Far more interesting is the ultimate attention-getter, death.

Surely this is an exaggeration. It is fantastic to suggest that our more open attitude to sexual activity really contains the seeds of our destruction. There simply is no logical reason to assume that our attitudes about sex and marriage are related to our development and acceptance of war, nuclear war in particular. Yet I suggest that we have accepted in our sexual ethic a life-denying anger at ourselves, which becomes the breeding ground of war.

For example Robert Heilbroner in his *Inquiry into the Human Prospect* quotes a distinguished professor of political economy at the University of London:

> Suppose that, as a result of using up all the world's resources, human life did come to an end. So what? What is so desirable about an indefinite continuation of the human species, religious convictions apart? It may well be that nearly everybody who is already here on earth would be reluctant to die, and that everybody has an instinctive fear of death. But one must not confuse this with the notion that, in any meaningful sense, generations who are yet unborn can be said to be better off if they are born than if they are not.[3]

Stated so boldly, we may find ourselves shocked by such an attitude, but in fact such a view has now become part and parcel of our lives. Certainly sex can be, and probably is, a form of play, but when that is all sex is, then we literally are playing with our death.

Even if there is a closer connection than we would like to think between our willingness to kill and our sexual ethics, what can we possibly do about it? We can at least begin by recapturing the obvious: Let there be lust. Thank God that we are created to be lustful people bent on copulating for the glory of God's creation. For in that lust lies not only the seeds of our future but our best chance for peace. As Christians we are a lustful people who know full well that we live in a troubled world, but who are sustained by a hope that refuses to let death have sway over us. For us there can be no denial of the life-giving opportunity offered by our lust, for through our community's provision of marriage our lust is given a form that manifests our faith in the power of God's kingdom of peace.

Let there be lust.

Yet surely this is wrong. The Church has thought it was following Matthew by condemning lust as the equivalent of adultery. But exactly the lust condemned is that which is life denying, that which is secret, that which is destructive of the community. The community of the New Age is not one that lives against nature, but rather one that makes possible our living naturally. It is natural that the wolf should dwell with the lamb. It is natural that a suckling child can put her hand in the adder's den. It is natural that we can be called to form a life with another person that makes possible the begetting of new life. It is natural that such life is the basis of a community that not only avoids killing but requires that we reconcile with those who anger us. Our reading of Matthew does not deny that we are people of anger and lust, but rather that we have now been given the means to free anger and lust from serving the powers of destruction and death.

We are no longer subject to destruction because this man Jesus—through his life, death, and resurrection—has made possible a community of the New Age. By learning to follow him, we are able to live transformed lives, no longer subject to the powers of the old age. Thus we have been given one another in marriage so that our secret desire for death might be transformed into life-giving and affirming action. We have no reason to fear ourselves or one another, as we no longer fear our destiny. Our destiny has been determined for all time through Jesus' resurrection. We thus have the confidence to pledge ourselves to one another in a way that makes it inconceivable that we would not wish to welcome new life from such a union. Such hospitality may come in the form of "biological" or "adopted" children—a distinction for which Christians have little use. So let us be a people of lust, for in that lust lies the peace that our world seems so tragically determined to reject.

15

The Water to Drown the Fire

Genesis 9:8-17
1 Peter 3:18-22
Mark 1:9-15

The story of the rainbow in Genesis 9 is a comfort. Especially during Lent—when we are required to dwell on our sins, to examine our life, to repent, and do penance—it is good to direct our attention to a beauty that is almost magical. For no matter how bad a mood we may be in, or how tired we may be, rainbows have the capacity to elicit from us a sense of joy and celebration. Each of us has a favorite story about the appearance of a rainbow. Moreover, I suspect that part of our positive response to rainbows, even for the most secular among us, is made possible because rainbows have been storied by this story. God has promised never again to destroy the earth by floods, and there in the sky, a sky that can often appear angry, we see the sure sign of that promise. So during Lent when we hold up our sins, when we prepare ourselves to witness the crucifixion, when we are trained to look without illusion at the terror of the world, it is good to know that no matter how terrible our sins—as individuals, as nations, or even as a species—God has forever promised not to destroy us because of those sins, not even for the Holocaust against his chosen people.

Moreover, one of the nice things about the covenant that the rainbow signifies is that it is with all creation—not just between God and humanity. It is the covenant between God and the earth—every living creature, grass, trees, rocks, and I guess even armadillos. In this day when we have become ecologically conscious it is nice to know that these ancient stories have contemporary relevance. Our lives as humans are bound up with all life, and our God is about the protection of all life—even armadillos. God's bow, which once no doubt was a bow of war, has been forever unstrung as a bow of death and placed in the sky to remind us and God—for it seems that God, too, needs a reminder—that God has promised never again to destroy God's creation. It is the loveliest of symbols.

And that, after all, is what we think—namely, the rainbow is a symbol engendered by this imaginative and engaging story. After all, we do not really believe that there ever was such a flood. No doubt, in the ancient Near East, folks may have thought a localized flood covered all the earth, at least all the earth they knew, but we know that there has never been a flood that covered all the earth at the same time. More important, however, is our conviction that God on balance is not the kind of God that would actually seek to destroy everyone and everything through the flood. Saving eight people and two of every kind is not sufficient to justify such destruction, no matter how bad the sin. To think otherwise is like trying to find some positive good in Hitler's destruction of the Jews. We believe that our God is in the business of life, not death. Therefore, we simply refuse to believe that humans, past or present, could do anything so terrible to justify his slaying them. So the rainbow for us is a sign of God's eternal goodwill rather than God's attempt to remind himself that he has pledged not to do it again.

Yet, when the rainbow becomes such a symbol, it cannot

> *For even if we do not believe that God has the will or the power to destroy the earth, we know damn well that we do.*

help seeming hollow and false. For even if we do not believe that God has the will or the power to destroy the earth, we know damn well that we do. Now the destruction will come not by water but by a fire that will leave no life untouched. There will be no arks this time by which even eight will be saved. Even if some are able to bury themselves in the earth's bowels for their forty days and nights, on returning to the surface they will only wish that they had been fortunate enough to have died instantly. For this time we have found the means of destruction for which there is no escape—the colors in this fire will be even more brilliant than those in the rainbow, but our eyes having been turned to ashes, we will not be able to behold that brilliance.

Some among us, the stern-minded, may suggest that God's hand is not absent in such fire. After all, God did not promise never again to destroy all life. God merely promised not to do it by a flood of water. God has kept that promise, but a wily God has found a way around the conditions set by the rainbow. This time God has found a way to destroy through the very presumptions of God's creatures. For our danger comes from our presumption that we can assume the stance of God by developing the power to destroy ourselves. Hating God, we pretentiously claim that we are self-creators because we can be our own destroyers. We prefer to commit mass suicide rather than to acknowledge that we are creatures of a gracious God. God thus uses the creation of our presumption, the embodiment of our strange self-hate, as the means of our own destruction.

We, of course, draw back from such interpretations, preferring to leave that kind of talk to backwoods preachers who have not had the disadvantage of a theological education. As a result, however, we really do not believe that God is up to much in our time. God is a handy symbol, like the rainbow, that all this will amount to something, that ultimately in the midst of all this confusion our lives have meaning, but God really does not mess around in matters involving nations and empires. Thus we really do not believe that God has much stake in history—or at least it is not the kind of stake that would result in the destruction of all life.

But as a result, we have trouble hearing the Gospel of Mark. To us it sounds like the same old thing—we ought to repent so we can live better lives, so we can help make the world more peaceful, less susceptible to nuclear destruction, and so on and so on. That's the

> *And what does apocalyptic mean except that God is once again acting decisively?*

ticket—only during Lent we ought to really try. But if we are to believe Mark's Gospel, that is not the message Jesus brought. For it seems that Jesus' call—the time is fulfilled, the kingdom of God is at hand, repent and believe the gospel—is apocalyptic. And what does *apocalyptic* mean except that God is once again acting decisively?

Notice, for example, what an odd list of events Mark gives us—Jesus is baptized and tempted; John is arrested; and Jesus comes out preaching, "Repent for the kingdom of God is at hand." John is arrested—how odd, yet on that event it seems the universe turns. That event drove Jesus into the public arena, making clear that God again is in the business of floods. Jesus comes announcing that the time of decision is upon us, requiring us to once and for all decide to be for or against God's kingdom. Nuclear weapons in the first century would not have made his message any more urgent. For what is decisive is not that we have the power to destroy the world, but that God's Messiah is now present among us, the kingdom is here, and we must repent if we are to be part of the kingdom.

In fact the only thing that makes such a call to repentance intelligible is that in fact the New Age is aborning. For this kingdom promises to make us a new people, a people no longer held captive by the powers of the world. For as we are told in 1 Peter, Christ died for our sins so that he might bring us to God. Indeed we are told that Christ even went to prison to confront the powers that reign, so that now even they are capable of obeying. They, too, were made his subjects through his resurrection—no power can stand against that power. But the Good News is that we have been graciously invited to be part of that victory by repenting and thus receiving a clear conscience—that is, a conscience that is no longer dominated by the fears that we have created through our pretensions to be our own creator.

God has renewed again his covenant with all the earth—he has given us a new and brilliant rainbow. It is the rainbow of God's patience; it is the very form of God's memory, through which we learn that God wills not only not to destroy us, but that he has gone so far as to offer us his salvation. This time the rainbow took the form of his Son, a concrete man, who cannot be made into just another symbol. Rather, he is God's presence who continues through his resurrection to offer us the alternative of life through baptism into this new time, this New Age. For in this water of baptism is the only hope we have of drowning the fire that threatens to engulf us all. In this water—in which we die, only to be reborn—do we have the basis to challenge the sinful presumption that we have the power to destroy God's creation. In this water we know that jailing John could not prevent the coming of God's kingdom but instead only marked the time of its beginning. In this water, and this water alone, do we find God's new flood that no longer destroys but makes well.

So the time is fulfilled, much is at stake, let us repent:

- Repent of our presumption that we, not God, rule;
- Repent of our presumption that we live at a time like all time;
- Repent of our attempt to substitute sentimentalities and causes for the proclamation of the gospel;
- Repent of our conceit of being happy to be American, male, or female;
- Repent of our unwillingness to be a baptized people, thus robbing the world of the means of knowing God's kingdom;
- Repent of our acting as if it matters little whether people are baptized or not;
- Repent of our unbelief that in Jesus of Nazareth God has forever changed our world.
- Repent, finally, of our unbelief that our repentance has nothing to do with the destiny of the universe.

As a people who have so repented let us come to the Table, a table made possible by our father Noah's willingness to trust in God's promise, trusting that God's covenant with the earth remains. But let us also remember through what we do at the Table, God creates the ark on which our, and the world's, salvation rests. For the Table of the Lord floats on the water of Jesus' baptism, thus making visible God's New Age. In the Meal, God says again—the time is fulfilled—and we again confess our unbelief but rejoice that God has overcome our sin. So let us rush to the Table to eat again with the Lord, thus making a witness to the world that God has promised our salvation. Even if the fire comes, and it may, we ask as Christian people that we will have enough time to enjoy the Meal of the New Age—trusting in God's promise that here is our destiny.

16

Resurrection, the Holocaust, and the Obligation to Forgive

Job 42:1-6
Acts 5:12a, 17-22, 25-29
John 20:19-31

So what do we do now? We have had our resurrection, our Easter. It was a grand time—the high point of the Church year liturgically, spiritually, and aesthetically. But what do we do now? Many of us feel emotionally drained and are not sure that we want to go on to the next step. Indeed we are not even sure that we know what the next step should be. Resurrection, after all, is a hard act to follow, for nothing seems capable of topping that one. Its dramatic nature seems to wash out anything that might follow.

We should not, therefore, feel surprised that we experience something of an emotional letdown after Easter. But I suspect that our inertia has more profound roots than simply coming down from a liturgical and emotional high. For resurrection, in spite of all the significant theological claims we make about it and what many of us may well think we believe about its significance, seems more like a retreat than a victory. We claim that through the resurrection God has done marvelous things for us, but in fact, we feel that God has left us holding the bag with few resources to know how to go on. In our day, resurrection, rather than being the supreme claim that God remains with us, seems to symbolize that just when the going gets tough—that is, just when we have to face the hard reality of having to go on living day by day—God takes a hike. Resurrection may not be good news, but bad news about the God that could not take it. God has escaped from our lives, leaving us with sentimental advice that it would certainly be a good thing if we loved one another.

Resurrection, as the felt absence of God from our lives, seems particularly powerful when we must face the Holocaust. All those who (previously) celebrated the absence of God as providing the space and

> *Resurrection, as the felt absence of God from our lives, seems particularly powerful when we must face the Holocaust.*

arena for human freedom have run aground on this reality. We live in a world where six million Jews and other "nondesirables" were put to death by people not too unlike you and me. How are we to "explain" that one? For like evil itself, every explanation seems to trivialize the reality. Who can blame God for exiting from this kind of world? I do not particularly want to be involved with it either.

But I am involved with it. I am the inheritor of the history and the benefits of a civilization that brutally and with cold-blooded efficiency put six million people to death. And like Job we cry out for an explanation—how and why could this happen to your own, and why and how could it be perpetrated in a culture formed by those who claim to worship the same God as the Jews? And, like Job, all we feel we get back is claims of power and incomprehensibility made all the more unsatisfactory by being packaged in magnificent poetry:

> "Look at Behemoth,
>> which I made just as I made you;
>> it eats grass like an ox.
> Its strength is in its loins,
>> and its power in the muscles of its belly.
> Its makes its tail stiff like a cedar;
>> the sinews of its thighs are knit together.
> Its bones are tubes of bronze,
>> its limbs like bars of iron." (Job 40:15-18)

And so it goes—on to the Leviathan. And so, like Job, we shut up. But we are not very happy with our silence. Job claims he now despises his doubt because where once he only had heard God, now he sees God, but that hardly seems satisfactory. Indeed, we feel that we no longer see God—in either Behemoth or Leviathan—as God took a dip into history, found it rather rough, and made a dramatic exit.

Job makes us particularly sympathetic with Thomas and his demand to "show me." Like Thomas, especially after Auschwitz, we want to see some marks that God has not abandoned us in this mess, for Auschwitz seems to be the surest sign we have that this is exactly what has happened. Where is God in this? Or even more radically, if God is in this how can we possibly continue the presumption that such a God is worthy of worship? Elie Wiesel describes the hanging of a young boy in his classic *Night:*

> One day when we came back from work, we saw three gallows rearing up in the assembly place, three black crows. Roll call. S.S. all round us, machine guns trained: the traditional ceremony. Three victims in chains—and one of them, the little servant, the sad-eyed angel.
>
> The S.S. seemed more preoccupied, more disturbed than usual. To hang a young boy in front of thousands of spectators was no light matter. The head of the camp read the verdict. All eyes on the child. He was lividly pale, almost calm, biting his lips. The gallows threw its shadow over him.

This time the Lagerkapo refused to act as executioner. Three S.S. replaced him.

The three victims mounted together onto the chairs.

The three necks were placed at the same moment within the nooses.

"Long live liberty!" cried the two adults.

But the child was silent.

"Where is God? Where is He?" someone behind me asked.

At a sign from the head of the camp, the three chairs tipped over.

Total silence throughout the camp. On the horizon, the sun was setting.

"Bare your heads!" yelled the head of the camp. His voice was raucous. We were weeping.

"Cover your heads!"

Then the march past began. The two adults were no longer alive. Their tongues hung swollen, blue-tinged. But the third rope was still moving; being so light, the child was still alive. . . .

For more than half an hour he stayed there, struggling between life and death, dying in slow agony under our eyes. And we had to look him full in the face. He was still alive when I passed in front of him. His tongue was still red, his eyes not yet glazed.

Behind me, I heard the same man asking:

"Where is God now?"

And I heard a voice within me answer him:

"Where is He? Here He is—He is hanging here on this gallows. . . ."

That night the soup tasted of corpses.[1]

Little good are tales about Behemoths and Leviathans when faced by this. And we are not sure what good it would do to be able, like Thomas, to touch nail holes and that wounded side.

However this gospel is familiar, and we feel sure that we know how to read it. As I suggested, we closely identify with Thomas because we assume that the issue is one of belief, and we think that we might be better believers—in spite of the commendation for those who have believed without having seen—if we could just get some better evidence. Behemoths and Leviathans do not serve us well as such evidence because we have been schooled to want to know historically that Jesus was really what the gospel seems to claim. Like Thomas we want some good first-hand evidence.

But of course this way of understanding the text is to misread it entirely. The issue was not one of belief at all—not in Jesus or his resurrection. John was well aware that such "evidence" was hardly convincing. For example, Jesus had raised Lazarus from the grave, but immediately after, John tells us, "Many of the Jews, therefore, who had come with Mary and had seen what Jesus did, believed in him. But some of them went to the Pharisees and told them what he had done" (John 11:45-46). Seeing is hardly believing.

At issue in Thomas's demand is not merely evidence. Notice the incompatibility of his confession with the evidence. For after Jesus shows him his hands and side, Thomas exclaims, "My Lord and my God!" Now that is an extraordinary deduction on the basis of the evidence. Resurrection, after all, does not prove lordship, but rather resurrection and the marks of crucifixion show that the resurrected Lord is not different from the crucified Lord. And in John's Gospel it is in the crucifixion that we see our Lord exalted. In the resurrection we learn that our crucified Lord remains with us even now.

> *Resurrection, after all, does not prove lordship, but rather resurrection and the marks of crucifixion show that the resurrected Lord is not different from the crucified Lord.*

To know that Jesus is the Lord comes not from seeing

nail holes, for we are only able to see the nail holes in a resurrected Lord for the simple reason that, like Thomas, we have first learned to follow this Lord and thus have been trained to know how he wills to be present. Namely, he is the Lord whose presence provides forgiveness and creates a community of forgiveness, for if we have received the Holy Spirit, his continuing presence, he tells us that we have the power to forgive sins. And we have such power because, through his cross and resurrection, we know we have been forgiven. No small matter, to be sure, for it is exactly the power of God that allows us to allow ourselves to be forgiven—much more than to forgive.

Note how different this presence is from that of the incomprehensibility of the God that creates the Behemoths—what is incomprehensible is not the power, but the power that forgives. So in effect, the schooling that Thomas must undergo is not unlike the schooling that we must undergo in the face of Auschwitz. Like Thomas, we seek a God of power that will make the horrible reality of the Holocaust come out right, but all we find is a God whose presence and power resides in his steadfast graciousness. Such a presence is easily trivialized, but when properly accepted it has a power that scares the wits out of the world, for the world does not seek to be forgiven, but to be in control by pretentiously assuming that it has the power to forgive.

In preaching this message of forgiveness, Peter found himself imprisoned. All that Peter said was:

> "The God of our ancestors raised up Jesus, whom you had killed by hanging him on a tree. God exalted him at his right hand as Leader and Savior that he might give repentance to Israel and forgiveness of sins. And we are witnesses to these things, and so is the Holy Spirit whom God has given to those who obey him." (Acts 5:30-32)

Like Peter we can end up in prison, when we find that we and the world want not a God with the power to forgive, but rather a God simply with power. We want a God that makes it possible to ensure "never again" when faced with Auschwitz. All we get is a God that calls us to be forgiven. For that, in short, is the heart of the gospel—namely, that we have been forgiven for the Holocaust. Resurrection is not God's retreat from us, but rather the clear sign that nothing we can do can alienate us from his steadfast will to forgive and love us and thus to make us into a people capable of forgiving and loving.

Wait a minute! Forgiveness is not the message we want when faced with Auschwitz. There are at least two objections to putting the matter this way. First, many feel they do not need to be forgiven for the Holocaust. After all, there have been worse genocides in history. All this talk about the uniqueness of the Holocaust is but another way that the Jews are reasserting their uniqueness. And of course there is some truth to that, but indeed that is exactly why the Holocaust is so significant—it happened to the Jews, God's chosen people, in the midst of an ostensibly Christian civilization.

But even the degree of the crime is not a peculiarly significant fact. You and I did not do it. We Christians in America did not do it. Indeed we fought to undo it. The attempt of many to claim responsibility for Auschwitz, or now for the evils of slavery, is but a masochistic way to secure moral identity through guilt in a morally confused civilization. And again there is some truth to that, but not very much. We simply cannot avoid, as Christians, recognizing the fact that we prepared people for the Holocaust for centuries. Who can listen after Auschwitz to the Johannine crucifixion account on Good Friday with its constant referent to "the Jews did this" and "the Jews did that" without feeling uncomfortable? Yet we must go on reading those passages as they are ours, and the Scripture must continue to remind us what havoc and evil they have wrought, culminating in the Holocaust. And by remembering, we also know why we so need to be forgiven for what happened there.

The second and even more substantive difficulty of seeing forgiveness in the aftermath of Auschwitz comes from its survivors. Surely from their perspective Christian talk about forgiveness in connection with Auschwitz is nothing less than obscene. What gall and pretension! First the Christians kill and persecute the Jews, and then they turn around and claim that God has forgiven them of such heinous crimes—not only forgiven them, but now they can learn to forgive themselves. The Jews should rightly feel that such forgiveness is surely cheap grace, but nonetheless that is what we must say. To say anything less would be to obey men and not God and thus be robbed of the presence of the Holy Spirit.

What gall and pretension! First the Christians kill and persecute the Jews, and then they turn around and claim that God has forgiven them of such heinous crimes—not only forgiven them, but now they can learn to forgive

Indeed Christian complicity in the Holocaust is due to our forgetting that our task was to obey God and not men. Our task is not to form a civilization where we would be safe from being thrown in jail for preaching God's forgiveness, but rather our task is to be a community of the forgiven. Such a community knows that God chooses not to rule the world by power divorced from love, but rather comes to us as the crucified Lord who remains ever ready to forgive—even the Holocaust.

I do not pretend that this message can be or should be easily accepted by Jew or Christian, but it is the message of the gospel. But I am afraid that the claim is finally even more offensive than this. Indeed, I hesitate to say it and certainly would try to avoid it if I were not under the discipline of the gospel. The resurrection not only means that we Christians have an obligation to accept forgiveness for the Holocaust, but we must ask the Jews to forgive us. If we do not do so we cannot help being caught in the eternal game of "I am guiltier than you" and thus fail to face our common destiny.

Questions of whether the Jews should be converted pale next to this, for our task is not to make Jews Christians but simply to ask them to forgive us. We must do that because we believe that we worship the same God, who in Christ has asked nothing new that had not already been asked of the Jew and the non-Jew. Just as the Jew has so often been forced to see God in the face of the stranger, so we must ask the Jew to see their God in us, the Christian—a God who asks of them and of us that we be capable of forgiveness.

The reality of the Holocaust cannot be made to go away by continuing to weigh guilt and responsibility. Such exercises, while not completely pointless, often come close to being obscene. Rather, we and the Jews must remember. But without forgiveness, we Christians are tempted simply to forget or deny, and Jews are tempted to lose their humanity in humiliation or vengeance. But if we are forgiven, we have the chance to remember and to make this terrible event part of our common history as we each look forward to the day when God's kingdom will come and we can embrace as brother and sister.

In the meantime, we can celebrate God's presence—the presence of the Spirit among us—by learning how to allow ourselves to be forgiven. We cannot very well march up to our Jewish neighbors and ask them to forgive us if we have created no other significant ties with them. With some imagination we can think of ways to let them appreciate how we—as "Easter people"—live by a new life, not in triumph, but in our openness to the suffering that has been theirs and is part of our history as well. In this way, we can begin a new journey together—with this week as a new beginning.

Notes

1. Taking the Bible Away from North American Christians

1. *The Journal of Kierkegaard*, translated, selected and with an introduction by Alexander Dru (New York: Harper & Row, 1958, p. 150). I am indebted to Allen Verhey for calling my attention to this quotation.

2. For a similar contention see William H. Willimon, *Shaped by the Bible* (Nashville: Abingdon Press, 1990), pp. 22-33.

3. We often overlook the immense changes that literacy occasions for the way we perceive ourselves in our world. I have no nostalgia for pre-literate cultures, though I do not think they were morally deficient for being pre-literate, but rather the challenge for Christians is to critically discern the significance of widespread literacy for the upbuilding of our community. For a fascinating discussion of the significance of literacy for Africa see Kwame Anthony Appiah, *In My Father's House: Africa in the Philosophy of Culture* (New York: Oxford University Press, 1992). As Appiah observes, "given the orality of traditional culture, it is possible to see how the accommodative approach can be maintained. With widespread literacy, the image of knowledge as a body of truths always already given cannot survive. But the recognition of the failures of constancy of the traditional worldview does not automatically lead to science; there are many other contributing factors. Without widespread literacy it is hard to see how science could have got started: it is not a sufficient condition for science, but it seems certainly necessary. What else, apart from a lot of luck, accounts for the beginning of modern science? So many things: the Reformation, itself-dependent not merely on literacy but also on printing and the wider dissemination of the Bible and other religious writings, with this transfer of cognitive authority from the Church to the individual; the experience with mechanism, with machinery, and agriculture and warfare; the development of universities. My claim is not that literacy explains modern science; it is that it was crucial to its possibility. And the very low-level of its literacy shaped the intellectual possibilities of pre-colonial Africa" (pp. 130-31).

4. The juxtaposition of individual versus community is the creation of liberal political presuppositions that I am trying to challenge. I do not deny, given the power of liberal practices, that many feel captured by such alternatives. That is why no theory of "community" is sufficient. Required is a different set of practices that hopefully might be constituted by the Church. Without such an alternative I fear that liberal societies are all too susceptible to the allure of fascism.

5. For examples of a literary approach to the Bible see Gabriel Josipovici, *The Book of God: A Response to the Bible* (New Haven: Yale University Press, 1988). While I am quite sympathetic with Josipovici's attempt to read the Bible as a "book," I am not at all convinced by his formalist presuppositions. For those presuppositions draw on essentialist presuppositions about anthropology that I think are theologically doubtful. For example, he says, "the Christian order is one we find perfectly natural and easy to understand, partly because we ourselves, whatever our beliefs, have been conditioned by a Christian culture, and partly because it corresponds to a profound need in each of us for closure and for a universe shaped according to a clearly comprehensible story"

(p. 47). Ironically, in the name of reclaiming the biblical point of view, the necessity of the Bible being a book of a particular people is lost.

The same kind of tension I think runs through the *Literary Guide to the Bible*, edited by Robert Alter and Frank Kermode (Cambridge: Harvard University Press, 1987). They justify the literary approach to the Bible on grounds that "the general reader can now be offered a new view of the Bible as a work of great literary force and authority, a work of which it is entirely credible that it should have shaped the minds and lives of intelligent men and women for two millennia and more. . . . Indeed literary analysis must come first, for unless we have a sound understanding of what the text is doing and saying, it will not be of much value in other respects. It has been said that the best reason for the serious study of the Bible—for learning how to read it well—is written across the history of Western culture: see what happens when people misread it, read it badly, or read it on false assumptions" (p. 2). The problem with these claims is the assumption that there is a misreading that can be determined on the basis of the text in and of itself by someone called the "general reader." Exactly what Alter and Kermode do through their literary analysis of the Bible is assume that the Bible is separable from the community that has learned to have the Bible read for certain purposes such as helping us live faithfully as God's people which is made possible by the cross and Resurrection. I suspect not all "intelligent people" share that interest.

For incisive critique of this approach to the Scripture see Stephen Moore, *Literary Criticism and the Gospels: The Theoretical Challenge* (New Haven: Yale University Press, 1989). Moore's criticism exposes some of the lingering new critical presuppositions that have been behind the appeal to the narrative character of the Gospels. I confess to be guilty of some of the sins he so accurately criticizes in some of my previous work on narrative, which continued to underwrite "new critical" presumptions. Hans Frei makes fascinating reading in this respect. Whether Frei was ever able to give up assumptions of the method of the new critics is not easily determined. See, for example, his posthumous *Types of Christian Theology*, edited by George Hunsinger and William Placher (New Haven: Yale University Press, 1992). Frei is clear that "the literal reading" is a reading that has become a consensus within the Church, yet he still clings to the presumption that the text of the Scripture is somehow required for the truthful display of Jesus' identity (pp. 138-40). There can be no question that Frei was increasingly drawn to a more communal account of the place of the Scripture but unfortunately his untimely death robbed us of a sense of how this extraordinarily gifted man would have displayed that. For a very insightful discussion of Frei's position as well as sympathetic criticism of that position see Jim Fodor, " 'Reference' in Paul Ricoeur's Hermeneutical Theory and Its Implications for Assessing Theology Truth Claims" (University of Cambridge: Dissertation for the degree of Ph.D., 1990), pp. 108-35. Fodor suggests that Frei never left behind the formalist presuppositions of the new critics.

6. For a useful overview of hermeneutics see Werner Jeanrond, *Theological Hermeneutics: Development and Significance* (New York: Crossroad Books, 1991). Jeanrond provides a quite helpful history of development of hermeneutics and contemporary discussions, but I have very little sympathy with his own constructive position. For example, he says, "nobody in contemporary theology would wish to question the necessity of proper exegetical methods as far

as biblical interpretation is concerned" (p. 159). Yet that is exactly what I wish to question because I no longer trust the distinction between exegesis and eisegesis. For example, he says, "the simple appeal to tradition in favor of or against a particular ecclesial or theological position can never replace critical and faithful argumentation" (p. 166). That, of course, is a false alternative because appeals to tradition are argumentative appeals that have to say this or that for this or that reason. I fear the very contrast between "critical" readings and traditions that his book presupposes, exactly because something called "general human experience" is privileged for the former.

2. Stanley Fish, the Pope, and the Bible

1. Stanley Fish, *Is There a Text in This Class? The Authority of Interpretive Communities* (Cambridge: Harvard University Press, 1980), p. 6. Fish is criticizing himself in this respect, as earlier in his book *Surprised by Sin: The Reader in Paradise Lost* (Berkeley: University of California Press, 1967) he made appeals to "the experience of every reader" (p. 30). Fish's argument is not in any way an excuse not to attend closely to the text, as his reading of Milton wonderfully demonstrates. Rather it is his attempt through close reading to persuade us to read Milton as he has slowly learned to read Milton. For a very astute appreciation of Fish and his significance for the use of the Bible see Moore, *Literary Criticism and the Bible: The Theoretical Challenge*, pp. 108-130. Fish has quite wrongly been associated with deconstructionist theories because to the extent that those theories may reproduce formalist presuppositions, they present a problem for Fish. N. T. Wright calls attention to the similarity between deconstructive reading and readings of Scripture that insist that what the Bible says to me, now, is the be-all and end-all of its meaning. As Wright wryly observes, "There are some strange bedfellows in the world of literary criticism" (*The New Testament and the People of God* [Minneapolis: Fortress Press, 1992], p. 61). Among those working in biblical criticism I find the work of Wright and Richard Hays to be the most promising.

2. Fish, *Is There a Text in This Class?*, p. 13. Neither Fish, or I, want to deny all interest in authorial intention though we are not convinced it is something in the "mind." Questions of what a particular author may or may not have "meant" will be of use given different purposes of reading.

3. Appiah observes, "in the specific context of the history of 'literature' and its study, recent debates have also left us attuned to the ways in which the factitious 'excavation' of the literary canon can serve to solidify a particular cultural identity. The official constitution of a national history bequeaths us the nation, and the discipline of literary history, as Michael de Certeau has aptly remarked, 'transforms the text into an institution'—and so bequest us what we call literature. The late Raymond Williams once noted that as the term *literature* begins to acquire its modern semantic freight, we find a development of the concept of 'tradition' within national terms, resulting in the more effective definition of 'a national literature.' As I argued at the start of this essay, 'literature' and 'nations' could hardly fail to belong together: from the very start they were made for each other." *In My Father's House*, p. 59. For a wonderful account of the creation of "english" as a subject, see Terry Eagleton, *Literary Theory: An Introduction* (Minneapolis: University of Minnesota

Press, 1983). Eagleton observes, " 'New Criticism' was the ideology of an uprooted, defensive intelligentsia who reinvented in literature what they could not locate in reality," p. 47.

4. Werner Jeanrond, *Theological Hermeneutics*, p. 3.

5. Fish, *Is There a Text in This Class?*, p. 14.

6. Jeff Stout, "The Relativity of Interpretation," *The Monist* 69 (January 1986): 14.

7. "Dogmatic Constitution on Divine Revelation" in *Documents of Vatical II* (New York: Guild Press, 1966), pp. 117-18.

8. Ibid.

9. I sometimes put the matter in this way, "The great social achievement of Roman Catholicism is not the Papal Encyclicals, but what other church would have been able to keep the Irish and the Italians in the same church." It may not seem like a great achievement, but at least in principle the Pope has the power to prevent Italians and Irish from killing one another over national loyalties. It is sad that too often that potential is not exercised in fact. Of course the challenge of disunity for Roman Catholics is even more pressing since the church's obvious disunity is a theological challenge for them in a manner that it is not for most Protestants. The only reason Roman Catholics are in a better position than Protestants is because they have the office of unity, they know they have a problem. My positive appreciation of Roman Catholicism does not mean I take an uncritical view of much Catholic practice. Yet I think that theologically there are few matters that justify our continued separation. For example, see Robert Jenson, *Unbaptized God: The Basic Flaw in Ecumenical Theology* (Minneapolis: Fortress Press, 1992).

10. That the rise in the authority of Scripture in the form of canon occurred approximately at the same time as the rise of an ordained leadership in the Church is not sufficiently analyzed. For it may well be that the authority of scripture must be balanced by the authority of the ordained clergy. I am not sure how this point might be developed, since any account of the authority of Scripture requires a much more determinative account of different kinds of authority and their function in the Church. I owe this point to Dr. Bruce Kaye.

11. "Dogmatic Constitution on Divine Revelation," pp. 120-21.

12. Georges Florosky, *Bible, Church, Tradition: An Eastern Orthodox View* (Belmont, Mass.: Nordland Publishers, 1972), p. 47.

13. Ibid.

14. Ibid., p. 48.

15. Ibid. For a much fuller account of how orthodox theologians think about these matters, see Michael Cartwright, "Practices, Politics, and Performance: Toward a Communal Hermeneutic for Christian Ethics" (Ph.D. diss., Duke University, 1988), pp. 270-86. I owe many of the arguments I am trying to develop here to Cartwright's work.

16. G. Ernest Wright, *The Biblical Doctrine of Man in Society* (London: S.C.M. Press, 1954), p. 21.

17. For example, see the essays in *Biblical Hermeneutics in Historical Perspective* edited by Mark S. Burrows and Paul Rorem (Grand Rapids: William B. Eerd-

mans, 1991). The essays by Burrows, Steinmetz, and McKee are all particularly pertinent. For example, McKee in her, "On Relating Calvin's Exegesis and Theology" observes, "what distinguishes Calvin, and gives his theology its impression of novelty, is the combination of a theological vision of unity and authority and practical applicability of Scripture, with unusual architectonic gifts. Calvin attempted to present a coherent picture of revelation by building theology out of exegesis and guiding exegesis by theology. Nothing in Scripture might be admitted without a reason, everything must fit together in a way that honors God and edifies the Church. In this process exegesis could shape theology and interpretation. More often, perhaps, theology molded exegesis. This might free some biblical text to be heard anew. For example, the focus on justification by faith and the priesthood of believers led to the acceptance of ordination for the temporal office of serving tables in Acts 6 and the inclusion of laity in the government of the church in Matthew 18" (p. 225). For a careful account of the complexity of Luther's and Calvin's view of the authority of Scripture, see B. A. Gerrish, *The Old Protestantism and the New: Essays on the Reformations Heritage* (Chicago: University of Chicago Press, 1982), pp. 51-68. In a letter to me, Reinhard Hutter reminds me that *solo scriptura* is an ecclesial and ecclesiological claim. "The Reformation *sola scriptura* does not make the Church superfluous; rather it implies the Church since it functions as intra-ecclesial criterion, something very different from later, banalized 'thin' version of *sola scriptura.* You could also call it a 'churched' principle which is played out against the domination of a reified traditionalism and points to that authority to which all conflicting parties have to submit and to that ground on which all conflicting parties have to stand." Hutter asks, therefore, "Which *sola scriptura?* Whose heresy?" to remind me the danger of a theologian trying to function as the *magisterium.*

18. Gerhard Ebeling, *The Word of God and Tradition* (Philadelphia: Fortress Press, 1968), p. 136. I am indebted to Dr. Philip Kenneson for calling Ebeling's book to my attention. John Milbank makes the astute point that Wilhelm Dilthey, "despite his grasp of the primacy of interpretation and the beginning of a sense of the temporality of all understanding, his hermeneutic methodology remains focused as capturing with precision the original moment of spiritual action or construction. It is this focus, indeed, which permits the claim that history has a 'scientific' objectivity. In fact, the concern to isolate and exactly describe a historic moment is, in one sense, a form of positivism. In the case of hermeneutics, this positivism is finally traceable to the exigencies of the Protestant *sola scriptura,* which, instead of a traditional accumulation of meanings, requires methodological guarantees that it can reproduce 'the original' and untrammelled word of God." *Theology and Social Theory: Beyond Secular Reason* (Oxford: Basil Blackwell, 1990), p. 79. Milbank's observation exactly characterizes Ebeling's position.

3. The Bible and America

1. Of course fundamentalism is not peculiar to North American Christianity, but I think the kind of fundamentalism with which I am concerned is peculiarly American. For a more global perspective that places fundamentalism within the general development of modernity see Bruce Lawrence, *Defenders of God: Fundamentalist Revolt Against the Modern Age* (New York: Harper & Row,

1989). Lawrence helpfully locates fundamentalism within structural developments in modernity, but I continue to doubt that "fundamentalism" is appropriately used to describe developments in Islam.

2. John W. Nevin, "The Sect System," in *Catholic and Reformed: Selected Theological Writings of John Williamson Nevin.* Edited by Charles Yrigoyen, Jr., and George H. Bricker (Pittsburgh: Pickwick Press, 1978), p. 139. It is fascinating to contrast Nevin's use of the word *sect* with more recent uses influenced by Troeltsch and Niebuhr. Sects for Nevin are characterized by their challenge to the unity of the Church; more recently *sect* means those who refuse to "act responsibly" for building a just society. Nevin's use of *sect* presumes that the Church is the predominant polity rather than recent use which presumes "real" politics is "out there." Again, I owe this point to Dr. Philip Kenneson.

3. Ibid., p. 139.

4. George Marsden, "Everyone's One Interpreter? The Bible, Science, and Authority in Mid-Nineteenth Century America," in *The Bible in America: Essays in Cultural History,* edited by Nathan O. Hatch and Mark A. Noll (New York: Oxford University Press, 1982), pp. 81-2. Charles Taylor in his *Sources of the Self: The Making of Modern Identity* (Cambridge: Harvard University Press, 1989) shows conclusively, I believe, how Bacon's perspective on science was shaped by the Puritan discovery of what Taylor calls the significance of "ordinary life," pp. 211-33.

5. George Marsden, *Fundamentalism and American Culture: The Shaping of Twentieth-Century Evangelicalism, 1870–1925* (New York: Oxford University Press, 1980), p. 112.

6. Nathan O. Hatch, "Sola Scriptura and Novus Ordo Secclorum," *The Bible in America,* p. 63. Hatch in his book, *The Democratization of American Christianity* (New Haven: Yale University Press, 1989) documents the close relationship between anti-clericalism and Alexander Campbell's claim for "the inalienable right of all laymen to examine the sacred writings for themselves" (p. 76).

7. Mark Noll nicely shows his connection in, "The Image of the United States as a Biblical Nation, 1776–1865," in *The Bible in America,* pp. 39-58.
    In a later essay, the "Bible in America," Noll notes, "Bible scholars, as good Americans, are usually friends of democracy and democratic impulses have been very important in the story of the Bible on these shores. Biblical scholarship, however, functions as a pontifical discipline, extraordinarily dependent on a small body of not quite infallible oracles, often German, whose conclusions serve to delimit the boundaries of normal science every bit as effectively as papal pronouncements did for Roman Catholics in bygone days. The incongruence of the privileged expert in a militantly democratic society is no new thing, but it is an incongruence with special meaning for Bible scholars in America. Students of the Bible's history, however, have barely touched the subject. Problems of conceptualization cannot, of course, be separated from problems of narration. Restricted perception of an object naturally restricts the ability to tell its story. For the history of the Bible in America two major conceptual difficulties are especially important. Put most directly, the difficulties are failures to admit that all Bible scholarship is dogmatic and that all Bible scholarship is political. To refine the issue, the problem is not so much the inability to see these realities as to explore their implications and to face up to their consequences." *The Journal of Biblical Literature* 106 (1987): 504.

The assumption that the Bible is crucial to culture as well as the nation is not simply to be found among conservatives. For example even George Lindbeck says "with the loss of knowledge of the Bible, public discourse is impoverished. We no longer have a language in which, for example, national goals (that is, questions of meaning, purpose, and destiny) can be articulated. We try to deal with apocalyptic threats of atomic and ecological disaster in the thin and feeble idioms of utilitarianism or therapeutic warfare." "The Church's Mission to a Postmodern Culture," *Postmodern Theology: Christian Faith in Pluralist World,* edited by Fredrick B. Burnham (San Francisco: Harper & Row, 1989), p. 47. Of course Lindbeck is right that such a culture will not produce Lincoln's Second Inaugural Address, but I am not inclined to think that more complete knowledge of the text by more people is going to make our culture better. Lindbeck seems to think that the mere knowledge of Scripture is a resource for a better polity. I remain quite unconvinced as few societies have had more people who knew the text of scripture than Germany. It did not provide much resistance to the Nazis. For a fuller account of Lindbeck's views on these matters see his, "Scripture, Consensus, and Community," *This World* 23 (Fall 1988), pp. 5-24. In this essay Lindbeck seems to want to have it both ways—namely as he puts it, "the Bible's community-forming role is not independent of community. It helps constitute the *ecclesia* only when interpreted communally in accordance with a community-constituting hermeneutic" (p. 8). In many ways I am very sympathetic to wanting to have it both ways yet not if as Lindbeck seems to suggest elsewhere that this means the text can be and should be "inteperted in its own terms" (p. 11).

8. Marsden, *Fundamentalism and American Culture,* pp. 220-21. In an odd way that is why Falwell thinks that unless we restore the Bible to the center of American life the family is doomed and if the family is doomed then the nation is doomed. That set of connections is exactly what Protestant liberals in the nineteenth century believed.

9. Ibid., p. 220.

10. David Steinmetz, "The Superiority of Precritical Exegesis," in *A Guide to Contemporary Hermeneutics: Major Trends in Biblical Interpretation* edited by Donald McKim (Grand Rapids: William B. Eerdmans, 1986), p. 65. This article first appeared in *Theology Today* 37 (April 1980): 27-38 and has been reprinted in David Steinmetz, *Memory and Mission* (Nashville: Abingdon Press, 1988), pp. 143-63. Steinmetz now indicates that the only change he would make in the article involves the description "precritical." To characterize all biblical criticism prior to the rise of historical criticism as "precritical" Steinmetz understands to be a mistake since there is nothing peculiarly uncritical about exegesis prior to the rise of historical criticism.

11. Ibid., p. 65.

12. Ibid.

13. Ibid., p. 66.

14. Krister Stendahl, "Biblical Theology: Contemporary," *Interpreters Dictionary of the Bible,* Volume I (Nashville: Abingdon Press, 1962), pp. 418-22.

15. Ibid., p. 422. For a wonderful analysis of Stendahl's argument, see Ben C. Ollenburger, "What Krister Stendahl 'Meant'—A Normative Critique of

'Descriptive Biblical Theology,' " *Horizons in Biblical Theology* 8 (1986): 61-81. Also important is Ollenburger's article, "Biblical Theology: Situating the Discipline," in *Understanding the Word: Essays in Honor of Bernhard Anderson*, edited by James T. Butter, Edgar W. Conrad, and Ben C. Ollenburger in JSOT Supplement Series 37 (Sheffield: JSOT Press, 1985), pp. 37-61. Ollenburger nicely shows that much of biblical criticism has been committed to distinguishing that which is "universally true" in the Bible from that which is "merely temporal." Of course the "universally true" is not and cannot be dependent on a contingent witness, so why higher critics continue to privilege the Bible cannot be explained.

16. Ibid., p. 422. Of course the argument Stendahl makes in this article in fact does privilege one set of interpreters. They are those who are members of the academic guilds associated with the academic study of Scripture. Distinction between what it meant and what it means is absolutely crucial to preserve for those who now create a different kind of laity through their assumed "expertise." Fundamentalists, of course, have their own forms of scholarship which in their own way are as demanding as the historical critical method.

17. Garry Wills account of Robert Thieme in his *Under God: Religion in American Politics* (New York: Simon and Schuster, 1990) makes fascinating reading in that respect. (See pp. 152-64.) I realize that introducing the notion of class is to raise what Paul Fussell describes as a "touchy subject," *Class* (New York: Ballantine Books, 1983), pp. 1-11. Yet I think nothing more determines the politics of the Church today than the reality of class. Tex Sample's wonderful description of "hard living" people and their alienation from the Church is a powerful reminder of the role of class in the Church as well as American society. See *Hard living People and Mainstream Christians* (Nashville: Abingdon Press, 1993).

18. Athanasius, *Incarnation of the Word of God*, translated by a religious C.S.M.B., with an introduction by C. S. Lewis (New York: Macmillan Company, 1946), p. 96.

4. Political Preaching

1. Stephen E. Fowl and L. Gregory Jones, *Reading in Communion: Scripture and Ethics in the Christian Life* (Grand Rapids: William B. Eerdmans, 1991).

2. Michael Cartwright argues persuasively that it was Reinhold Niebuhr who created the politics that then produced the problem of how Scripture could be used ethically. If you want, as does Niebuhr, to privilege the realist discourse of liberal democratic polities in the name of sin, then as a matter of fact Scripture, and of course Jesus, is relevant only as the impossible possibility. See *Practices, Politics, and Performance: Toward a Communal Hermeneutic for Christian Ethics* (Ph.D. diss., Duke University, 1988), pp. 31-68.

3. Rowan Greer "The Christian Bible and Its Interpretation," in James Kugel and Rowan Greer, *Early Biblical Interpretation* (Philadelphia: The Westminster Press, 1986), p. 111.

4. Andrew Louth, *Discerning the Mystery: An Essay on the Nature of Theology* (Oxford: Clarendon Press, 1983), p. 112. In an interesting article "The Literal, the Allegorical, and Modern Biblical Scholarship," James Barr argues that biblical criticism is a form of allegory. He argues that what biblical critics are really trying to do is to get at the theological significance of these texts rather than to mine them for their historical meaning. However, he continues to hold the odd

view that what theology means is what is in the "ideas and minds of the writers of Scripture" (*Journal for the Study of the Old Testament* 44 [June 1989] 12).

5. For this view of allegories see David Dawson, *Allegorical Readers and Cultural Revision in Ancient Alexandria* (Berkeley: University of California Press, 1992). Dawson notes that Valentinus' reading of Scripture was a subversion of Judaism even more thorough than the Gnostics (p. 176). Dawson suggests that such subversion is the result of the virtual eradication of Alexandrian Judaism.

6. Dawson, *Allegorical Readers and Cultural Revision in Ancient Alexandria*, p. 2. For an interesting, and I think persuasive, account of exegesis as a form of rhetorical practice, see David Cunningham, *Faithful Persuasion* (Notre Dame, Ind.: University of Notre Dame Press, 1991), pp. 204-54.

7. For a fuller account of my understanding of the context of preaching, see William Willimon and Stanley Hauerwas, *Preaching to Strangers: Evangelism in Today's World* (Louisville: Westminster/John Knox Press, 1992).

8. For this sense of biblical essay, see John Howard Yoder, *He Came Preaching Peace* (Scottsdale, Ariz.: Herald Press, 1985), pp. 11-14.

9. For a fuller account of my theological critique of the family see *After Christendom* (Nashville: Abingdon Press, 1992).

10. Yet the issue remains, By what authority does Stanley Hauerwas preach? I am not ordained or commissioned by any ecclesial body to preach publicly or conduct worship services. Thus Reinhard Hutter asks, "Does not your very practice underwrite the assumption that anybody should be able to preach about any text in the Bible at any given time or if not anybody then at least the trained academic theologian?" Unless there is an answer to this question how can I ask the reader to read these sermons as anything more than private musing?

   I wish I had an adequate response to these questions. I can say that the sermons are a response to requests by appropriate ecclesial representatives and done under their direction. The sermons were not self-generated. But such a response fails to deal with the underlying problem that the very practice of using exhibits in this book contradicts the argument I have made. So when all is said and done we are left with a liberal exchange in which everyone gets to make up his or her own mind.

   The problem, of course, could not be resolved even if I were ordained because ordination unfortunately no longer signifies the right to exercise legitimate power. I sometimes suggest that the curricula of seminaries should be scrapped and each professor could teach whatever they wished as long as it centered around the question "Why can only those duly ordained preside at the eucharist?" I assume some might wish to answer that question negatively, but in doing so they would have to shape their theology in terms of ecclesial practice.

   I am tempted to try to answer the question of authority by developing theoretical accounts of authority. For example, I am particularly attracted to the work of Yves Simon, who distinguished between views of authority that asume the community is deficient, and those who assume authority is necessary because of the richness of gifts in a community that requires coordination. Yet such theories, while an aid for imagination, cannot supply the actual practice of authority we so desperately require.

   Some may assume, given the above argument, that I think our only recourse is to become Roman Catholic. I do believe that any attempt to do theology that fails to struggle day in and day out with that question cannot be serious. Of course it is not just the Roman Catholics who challenge those of us in the Protestant mainstream about these matters but also the practice of authority exercised by those who understand themselves to be "gathered communities." Ironically, our situation has made us realize that Roman Catholics and those labeled sectarians have more in common than their historical division would suggest. After all, the "hierarchical" nature of Catholicism is, at least in principle, the attempt to respect and enhance the authority of the gathered community. Yet the challenge facing us will not disappear by Protestants becoming Roman Catholics as we are caught in webs of power far too determinative to be overcome by ecciesial identification—though ecclesial identification might not be a bad place to begin resistance to those powers.

So finally all I can say in response to the question, By what authority? is that I am judged by my own work. Through such judgment I hope that we might all learn better how to imagine what it means to be under the authority of God's word.

5. The Insufficiency of Scripture

1. James Wm. McClendon, Jr., *Biography as Theology* (Nashville: Abingdon Press, 1974), pp. 127-28.

2. Vincent J. Donovan, *Christianity Rediscovered* (Maryknoll, N.Y.: Orbis Books, 1982), p. 127.

6. A Sermon on the Sermon on the Mount

1. Gene Davenport, *Into the Darkness: Discipleship in the Sermon on the Mount* (Nashville: Abingdon Press, 1988), p. 15.

2. Ibid., p. 88.

3. Anne Tyler, *Saint Maybe* (New York: Alfred A. Knopf, 1991), p. 122.

4. Richard Lischer, "The Sermon on the Mount as Radical Pastoral Care," *Interpretation* (April 1987), pp. 161-62.

5. Ibid., p. 163.

7. You Are Not Accepted

1. Paul Tillich, *The Shaking of the Foundations* (New York: Charles Scribners & Sons, 1948), pp. 161-62.

2. Ibid., pp. 157-58.

9. The August Partiality of God's Love

1. Wendell Berry, *Home Economics* (Berkeley, Calif.: North Point Press, 1987), pp. 112-22.

13. Hating Mothers as the Way to Peace

1. J. Glenn Gray, *The Warriors: Reflections on Men in Battle* (New York: Harper & Row, 1970), p. 40.

14. Lust for Peace

1. Jonathan Schell, *The Fate of the Earth* (New York: Alfred A. Knopf, 1982), pp. 157-58.

2. Ibid., pp. 171-72.

3. Robert Heilbroner, *An Inquiry into the Human Prospect* (New York: W. W. Norton, 1980), p. 180.

16. Resurrection, the Holocaust, and the Obligation to Forgive

1. Elie Wiesel, *Night* (New York: Bantam, 1980), pp. 75-76.